TRANSFER, MEMORY, & CREATIVITY

TRANSFER, MEMORY,

&

CREATIVITY

AFTER-LEARNING AS PERCEPTUAL PROCESS

GEORGE M. HASLERUD

UNIVERSITY OF MINNESOTA PRESS

MINNEAPOLIS

© Copyright 1972 by the University of Minnesota. All rights reserved.
Printed in the United States of America at the
George Banta Company, Inc., Menasha, Wisconsin.
Published in the United Kingdom and India by the Oxford
University Press, London and Delhi, and in
Canada by the Copp Clark Publishing Co. Limited, Toronto

Library of Congress Catalog Card Number: 72-79096
ISBN 0-8166-0656-0

To ETHLYN
*Whose Creativity
Has Enriched My Life
These Many Years*

PREFACE

Chapters on transfer in most texts for the psychology of learning or educational psychology must be described as perfunctory. They usually fail to emphasize the importance of the topic, to integrate transfer into the rest of psychology, and especially to indicate how it can aid application of knowledge. Since these three issues are the main themes of this book, it complements those works which develop primarily the input side of learning but leave dangling the all-important problems of the availability of what has been learned and of the generation of new alternatives to meet new situations. Its underlying concern is the relevance of learning.

Since Thorndike's pioneer experiments and writing on transfer at the beginning of this century, many have tried various combinations of identical elements to find a useful paradigm. If any other field showed as disappointing results as those portrayed in chapter I, one would suspect that it was in a cul-de-sac. Likewise the reactions against identical elements, e.g., Judd's principles and Gestalt organization, seemed promising until one asked for their specific directions on how to make the transferring values functionally applicable. In 1958 Travers could still write in his *Introduction to Educational Research,* "A major difficulty in the design of studies related to conditions affecting generalization of training stems from the lack of any particularly useful theory." English and English in their dictionary made the same complaint.

Many in psychology and education have admitted that transfer is at once the most important and the most neglected part of the psychology of learning. A fresh approach to the problem depends on a more adequate theory than has heretofore been provided. The development of my perceptual theory has come only through a lengthy gestation. The fundamental idea was conceived sixteen years ago during a sabbatical while falling asleep on the tatami mats of a Japanese inn. I had become concerned about the isolated hodgepodge of phenomena included under memory and transfer, the inadequacy of available theory, and the inability of many college graduates to apply their education to their work and personal life. A number of experiments and years later I was still wrestling with the problem. Then in 1968 during another sabbatical the resolution occurred on the banks of the Amazon in the jungle of eastern Peru. I began to see how a perceptual reorganization of the phenomena of after-learning (events after a criterion has been met) would lead directly to a fruitful hypothesis differentiating the conditions for literal and creative transfer.

This is a book of hypotheses built around a new construct, the Theater of Perception,* to provide integration and a theoretical basis for all after-learning. In a changing world especially important is the capacity to generate new alternatives, i.e., to exhibit creative transfer. Since nearly all the experiments and previous theories of transfer have been of the literal type, in chapter VII the creative, cognitive kind of transfer is given its own name, a neologism, *projecscan,* because of the entirely different perceptual process employed in finding new alternatives for problems that resist the old solutions.

Though this new perceptual theory shows promise of being use-

---

* Definitions for the constructs as well as other terms used in a special way related to the perceptual theory are in chapter XI, the most important being for "transfer" (literal transfer) and "projecscan" (creative transfer).

Three terms are capitalized to emphasize their use as theoretical constructs: Apperceptive Mass, Theater of Perception, and Perceptual Future.

ful as well as integrative, its validity eventually will depend on how well the deductions are supported by crucial experiments. In chapter XIV the theory is dissected and examined to point out where it is most vulnerable. Pedagogically this also helps a reader test his own understanding of the theory from a different perspective.

Rather than let a generation elapse between theory and application as often happens in science, chapter XIII begins making deductions from the theory. In relation to education, the theory makes clear why conventional examination procedures in schools and colleges largely preclude later creative development of alternatives for problem solution; why a teaching machine may be programmed for memory and the literal kind of transfer but not for the creative sort; why a well-stocked Apperceptive Mass is a necessary but not a sufficient base for creativity; why modern man needs a different kind of memory and retrieval skills. On the positive side, the theory provides a new rationale for the liberal arts and continuing adult education.

I hope this study interests three groups that have been kept in mind during the writing. First, those in psychology and education who will test experimentally and logically the adequacy of the new perceptual theory as an organizing principle for after-learning and whose interest may develop the theory and its implications further. Second, instructors and students in courses in psychology of learning and educational psychology who have realized how most texts on learning have neglected half the subject—the phenomena of after-learning. Third, citizens, teachers, and school and college administrators disturbed by the low rate of dividends on our present educational effort. From the theory, procedures may be worked out to increase the probability that the individual will maintain his educational level and be able to apply what he learns. The theory may make a contribution to the debate on what long-range gains in an educated man's competence could come from the study of liberal arts taught with the integration of learning and creative transfer in mind.

I thank the University of New Hampshire for three sabbaticals during which the theory took form; the Fulbright Commission for two stimulating years as a visiting professor in Japan and Peru and colleagues and students in those countries with whom I discussed the problem of transfer and after-learning; the participants in seminars on transfer at the universities of Lund and Uppsala in Sweden in 1961; the United States Department of Education for a two-year grant to test the value for transfer of given and derived principles, the results of which indicated to me that this had been a secondary issue and thus opened again my search for a more fundamental theory; Jerome Bruner, Harry Harlow, Wolfgang Köhler, Hobart Mowrer, Karl Pribram, and Edward Tolman, whose experiments and theories I consulted, and especially the books *Plans and the Structure of Behavior* and *The Senses Considered as Perceptual Systems*; my colleagues from departments throughout the university in the Behavior Seminar at the University of New Hampshire who helped me criticize two of my earlier formulations of a theory of transfer; my students in the psychology of learning and the integration of psychology, and graduate students in the seminar on perception at the University of New Hampshire during the last twenty-five years for their reactions and suggestions; former students Drs. George Harker, Gary Mitchell, Wallace Russell, and Duane Whittier for their special help in the development of early stages of the theory; the Central University Research Fund at the University of New Hampshire for a grant to carry through the concluding library research and the typing of the manuscript; and my wife Ethlyn for improving and inking the figures.

G. M. H.

Durham, New Hampshire
October 12, 1970

CONTENTS

TRANSFER, MEMORY, & CREATIVITY

I THE PROBLEM
IN AFTER-LEARNING

Trying to find the solution . . .
First, we have to
understand the problem.
G. Polya

The problem in after-learning is really a duality—how to make available what has been learned, and how to derive new alternatives that were not included in original learning.

After-learning includes the variety of behaviors in an individual after he has learned something specific to a given level; it can range from immediate memory to changes after graduation with a B.A. degree. The standards for the level required may vary from the just barely learned one perfect recital of a list in Ebbinghaus's experiments on himself to such high criteria as twenty-four errorless out of twenty-five trials in some of Lashley's experiments with rats. It can be argued that reaching a criterion is actually a manifestation of memory. No one would disagree that learning and memory are inextricably intertwined, but after the standard has been met, the regular learning efforts ordinarily stop, the learner turns to other activities, and the recovery of what had been learned becomes different from a mere repetition during the input.

Immediate memory has a future of only a few seconds. Within that time, however, the problems of availability of information from the perceptual field and the going beyond the information given are both subject to study and have practical implications.

A more extended future opens for those learning experiences

3

that somehow become part of longtime memory. As Miller, Galanter, and Pribram (1960) and others have realized, learning presents no real difficulty for organisms with complex nervous systems. Retrieval is the main problem. If what has been learned is unavailable, the question could well be asked, "Why learn?" Since obviously not all problems can be solved by immediate perception, memory must contribute its resources.

In a changing world, the second problem becomes as important as retrieval. The future no longer permits the expectation that solutions learned today will be pertinent tomorrow. One can empathize with an old Yale graduate of the class of "oughty-one" who told me with good humor but a note of sadness, "My education is obsolete!" The schools and universities cannot rest complacently when even one who had graduated finds himself over the years unable to apply his knowledge and to transfer understanding to new situations.

A difficulty little realized about knowledge is its growing incomprehensibility, even within the individual's own store, unless it is continually reinterpreted and renewed. The unwary and unprepared may wreck on the rocks of adaptation to the point of perceptual blindness or on the equally dangerous Charybdis of panic that one has no resources to meet strange and new problems, that nothing one has learned or experienced applies.

How well a science progresses can be estimated by its development of adequate theory. Without some ordering generalizations and conceptions, one may find only a collection of sundry observations and may experience real trouble in applying the knowledge beyond the empirical situation where it was developed. Microtheories may be all that is feasible for a certain state of development. However, too myopic a view may retard the insights that require an organic whole.

This book attempts to construct a more comprehensive theory than has been available hitherto in order to provide for both availability and new alternatives. Educational psychology has been estranged too long from the mainstream of development in the psychology of learning. But even the study of learning has been

4

impoverished by the artificial boundaries between it and the areas of perception, consciousness and unconsciousness, thinking, problem solving, and creativity. Especially neglected has been the search for an adequate theory of transfer. The main thrust of my book will be to assess past efforts in this direction and to develop a new theory based more realistically on a broad interrelated theory of after-learning.

The intimate relation between theory and practice and even a clear perception of what a field of investigation includes are well illustrated by the problem English and English (1958) had in defining transfer: "A general term for change in ability to perform a given act as a direct consequence of having performed another act relevant or related to it." As they go on to say, though, this definition does not separate transfer from fatigue, sensory adaptation, or stimulus generalization, nor does it clarify what makes the first task relevant to the second. Neither, we might add, does it distinguish between a literal transfer and a creative one. Nor does it indicate whether it is to the perception of the new task or only to its operation as a response that the transfer functions. English and English then contend that "the unsatisfactory nature of the above reflects the unsatisfactory state of theory."

Darwin (1959) in his autobiography told what a dramatic change in perception occurred after he had read Agassiz's theory of glaciation. "On this tour I had a striking instance of how easy it is to overlook phenomena, however conspicuous, before they have been observed by anyone. . . . neither of us saw a trace of the wonderful glacial phenomena all around us; we did not observe the plainly scored rocks, the perched boulders, yet these phenomena are so conspicuous that . . . a house burned down by fire did not tell its story more plainly than this valley."

With a fresh look at the phenomena of after-learning from a new theoretical stance, many puzzling oddities, e.g., the relation of memory and creativity, may fit into place and a more satisfactory definition of transfer be found than that of English and English.

A profound dissatisfaction with our educational system finally became vocal when the Sputniks jarred complacency. Admiral

5

Rickover testified, "I tried to get people to help me do a job in nuclear-power development, and I found the product of our schools quite unsatisfactory" (Rickover, 1959). For years college teachers have decried the preparation in the high schools, and the high schools in turn the lack of even adequate reading ability of graduates from grammar school. Many teachers would agree that prerequisites often do not make students readier for the next course.

Dr. Oscar Handlin of Harvard in a stimulating article entitled "Live Students and Dead Education" (1961) had this to say, "In fact, every college course of which I know begins from the beginning and takes for granted no previous knowledge of the subject. More than two decades of experience with the best-trained students in the country have convinced me that it would make no difference whatever if they never studied American history before they came to college." From the Air Force Studies Flanagan (1947) similarly reported, "In gunnery, especially, much of the work of the ground trainers seemed to have been largely wasted effort. In a few instances it was found that training actually produced interference so that untrained individuals were superior to the 'trained' ones."

Some who would admit the foregoing as an inevitable difficulty when trying to educate a general population would nevertheless claim results for what they term the educable minority. Are those especially selected or given opportunities yielding high educational dividends?

In the 1930s the famous Eight-Year Study of thirty preparatory schools, which were allowed to try out various curricula with the assurance that their recommended graduates would be accepted at colleges of their choice, had an extensive college follow-up of the graduates of the experimental and control schools. Chamberlin (1942) in his provocative book *Did They Succeed in College?* wrote, "These graduates of progressive schools have not set their schools on fire, as some progressives may have hoped they would ... according to the commonly used criteria of success in college, including grades and scholastic honors and participation and success in extracurricular activities, the progressive school graduates as a group came out *a little ahead* of a comparison group composed of traditionally trained students of closely similar scholastic aptitude and social and economic background." By the sophomore year the differences were almost indistinguishable in the over three thousand who were studied.

Similarly Conant (1957) observed, "As a matter of statistics the high school graduate does better than the private school boy in Harvard College though he may have considerable difficulty the first year." In New York City the results of segregating the bright into high-level schools have been disappointing. The special science high schools produced no more outstanding science students than did the regular high schools when ability was controlled as a variable (Shayon, 1959).

Follow-up studies are expensive and difficult, but there is no substitute for them when one is asking about outcomes. Pace and his associates, using an extremely well-constructed, interesting, and objective questionnaire, were able to get over 90 per cent return from several university classes after ten years. Summarized in *They Went to College*, the results raise questions about the value of a college education. Those with four years of college differed hardly at all in social, political, and other behavior from those with only one year. Except in income there was no significant difference in favor of the four-year group (Pace, 1941).

Some have given up general education as a preparation for an occupation or for even a college major and seem to despair of any useful transfer. The extensive training programs of the Air Force during World War II were evaluated by Flanagan (1947): "The conclusion from these findings is that a greater improvement can be gained in effectiveness in the activity for which the individual was selected and trained by research on selection and classification than by research on training procedures." He also stated that "one of the most important findings with respect to learning was the surprising degree of specificity of learning on ... apparently similar skills." But the strictly empirical approach must have been insufficient, for as late as 1961 the Army Research Office still wanted to develop concepts and principles in the field of transfer of training: "Current knowledge of conditions which influence the transfer of skill or knowledge acquired in one situation to its effective use in others is yet insufficient to guide the development of maximally efficient training programs in a variety of job areas. A transfer of training could be of considerable value in guiding further research in development of simulators and training devices as well as curriculum engineering."

The programming of problems for such devices as B. F. Skinner's automatic teaching apparatus probably represents the ultimate in nondependence upon transfer. Not even the transfer within a paragraph or topic is employed; the material to be learned is broken into "bits" or "steps" and the response to each is operantly conditioned. The one who makes the program is the only one who has to organize and relate.

The downgrading of transfer ever since the Thorndike and Woodworth experiments at Columbia seventy years ago, and support by experiments elsewhere, has been well summarized in Pressey and Janney (1937): "Much of what has been attributed to special types of education is really the result of selection [of learners]. When transfer occurs, it is not general but specific. . . . Training directly in a skill or ability appears always to be more efficient than training in another ability plus transfer to the ability it is desired to improve." Contemporaneity then, according to this view, would be the prescription for every school subject. However, Thorndike himself had this reservation: "Finally, it must be remembered that a very small spread of training may be of great educational value if it extends over a wide enough field. If a hundred hours of training on being scientific about chemistry produced only one-hundredth as much improvement in being scientific about all sorts of facts, it would yet be a very remunerative educational force" (Thorndike, 1913).

All schooling except the last, immediate, on-the-job training would, under a conception of extreme specificity of learning, be only schooling for the sake of schooling. Unless there is substantial transfer, the school curriculum might as well concern itself mostly with economical custodial care of students during daylight hours. Nor do those escape the problem of transfer whose interest is the development of social and moral capacities. The problem goes even deeper, for the old knowledge may often seem to have nothing in common with the new until someone calls attention to the similarities. Apparently old knowledge may be well learned and available when the exact cues used in learning elicit it but incomprehensible or absent if the cues are slightly different. Training for flexibility then is the only practical kind of training for a changing world.

Common is the lament that graduate schools are turning out specialists rather than the broadly educated teachers needed for the development of the next generation. At the root of this problem may be the neglect of transfer.

College catalogues are full of the prescribed curricula particularly in engineering, medicine, and other similar fields. The idea that the student must be taught or come in contact with each activity or process used in that field was pushed so far that the courses were expanded to include everything. Then began the fractionation of the field into minute specialties. The trouble was that the doctor of medicine found much of his practice consisted in psychosomatics and in lancing boils, leading to the cry that the practitioner was unprepared. Only after a time did the leading schools begin to explore, as though it were radically new, the value of a more general education. The engineer began to include the humanities and social sciences in his program of studies, not just as embellishments, but as a sound way of becoming educated for a demanding but uncertain future. The doctor too was not to get a smattering of all techniques to become a walking encyclopedia of medical knowledge but rather to become an educated man who was especially conversant with how to solve medical problems with the aid of sources he had learned to evaluate.

Even if the evidence were better that what was learned was available later, the question cannot be dodged that that kind of response may not be good enough for a dynamic, rapidly changing world. Whereas in primitive societies a specific technique can be

9

passed down from one generation to the next, modern man is confronted with the dilemma that his specific training may be obsolete by the time he gets to practice it. The doctor who learned the mastoid operation finds it unneeded with antibiotics available. The necessary fireman on a locomotive has no place on an automatic diesel train. Dr. Bronk, president of the Rockefeller Institute and the National Academy of Sciences, evaluating graduate work, commented in a lecture to the Centennial Convocation of Land Grant Colleges and State Universities in November 1961, "To train students to deal only with problems which can be conceived and defined now is to deny them the foundations for dealing with the unanticipated problems of a rapidly evolving future."

If we examine the arguments of educational critics, we find they do not propose the faster and faster rate of specific learning which might be the Thorndikian answer to the obsolescence problem. Instead, the critics go back to "training the mind," or more technically, to formal discipline.

Admiral Rickover, whose talent in applied nuclear engineering is uncontested, has diagnosed and prescribed for education in the United States in these terms: "Anyone who has tackled a difficult subject, such as higher mathematics, and used it to solve complicated problems, knows he has emerged from the experience with a mind that functions better. Thereafter he will find it easier to tackle other subjects and other problems, because his mental capacity has grown" (Rickover, 1959). Compare this unequivocal statement of the assumptions of formal discipline with this dialogue from Plato's *Republic*:

"Again; have you ever noticed that those who have a turn for arithmetic are, with scarcely an exception, naturally quick at all sciences; and that men of slow intellect, if they be trained and exercised in this study, even supposing they derive no other benefit from it, at any rate progress so far as to become invariably quicker than they were before?"

"That is true."

"And I am pretty sure, also, that you will not easily find many sciences that give the learner and student so much trouble and toil as arithmetic."

Another critic, Dr. Arthur Bestor, a historian, in his *Restoration of Learning* (1955), had this to say: "An indispensable function of education, at every level, is to provide sound training in the fundamental ways of thinking represented by history, science, mathematics, literature, language, art, and other disciplines involved in the course of mankind's long quest for usable knowledge, cultural understanding, and intellectual power ... the particular contribution which the school can make is determined by, and related to, the primary fact that it is an agency of intellectual training." Bestor believes that certain subjects of study develop the intellect and have more than immediate value. Other subjects gain only his scorn for being a too contemporaneous "life adjustment" which has no transfer value.

Probably the best known modern critic of education is James Conant, former president of Harvard. Unlike some other ciritics he has organized extensive surveys of the senior and junior high schools and the teachers colleges, and has through observation, interview, and comparative measurement attempted to discover the causes of the lack of excellence in education and has made recommendations for improvement. He would not, like Rickover, take the French *lycée* or the German *Gymnasium* as his educational model. However, the accumulation by the student of a certain background of courses is emphasized, and little or nothing is said about the transfer or availability of this knowledge. Implicit is the idea that with the right subjects for students who are set for high goals and kept well motivated, the mind increases its power. Conant would encourage formal discipline by improving the curriculum.

Perhaps this is the point where we ought to examine why formal discipline lost out with psychologists well over a half century ago. Parenthetically one needs to add that Osgood (1953) concluded that the case against formal discipline was not yet closed. Faculty psychology (mind divided into discrete capacities and each located in a particular part of the brain) and its attendant formal discipline (the building up or restriction of each faculty) had received criticism from some like Herbart in the nineteenth century. But the classical languages and mathematics continued to hold their dominant place in the schools before 1900 because it was thought that the difficulty of mastering them developed "mental muscle" as physical exercise develops biceps. To the arguments that many pupils hated them and that they had no practical value, the supporters of these disciplines replied that the disagreeableness of the task made it even more valuable for mental development. The sciences edged their way into the curriculum by their proponents claiming that they too had value as formal discipline.

In chapter V the laboratory experiments by which Thorndike arrived at his theory of transfer by identical elements will be examined, but in the present chapter emphasis is placed on how he carried the attack against formal discipline into the schools. When a claim was made that Latin improved performance in English or in the study of geometry and logic, Thorndike and his students made controlled tests of these assertions. They verified that those taking Latin courses had higher grades in English; this would seem to support the claim of formal disciplinists. However, when Latin and non-Latin groups were paired according to an independent measure of intellectual ability, there was no significant difference between the groups. Selection, often self-selection, of those undertaking a particular kind of training was thus shown to be a much more important factor than the purported value for transfer of the specific subject.

Some Latin teachers like Rapp (1945) studied the evidence produced by Thorndike and others. Rapp agreed that Latin produced no automatic transfer but contended that the self-conscious "teaching for transfer" would make possible a rich transfer. Coxe (1924) had already made an extensive study of such effects as teaching the English cognates of Latin words and the principles of changing form from Latin to English. He found some value for transfer from the teaching of principles but less than expected for the teaching of cognates over that from traditional Latin classes. The outcome of this study was to show how hard it is to specify a priori what will be a good procedure for transfer.

"Teaching for transfer" has remained largely the realm for the "successful teacher," who often cannot tell precisely why his pupils are able to produce better in a new situation than the pupils of others. Lack of an adequate theory left the educational psychologists trying without significant success one training method after another, sometimes together in a shotgun approach. No one in education seems to have had the indefatigability of an Edison who tried over three thousand kinds of carbonized fibers before he found one that had the right properties for the filament of his electric light. However, even in Edison's laboratory his later assistants, recruited from the universities where they had learned chemical and physical theory, sometimes found occasion to demonstrate its value. Rosanoff described in an article in *Harper's* (1932) how he developed the new kind of wax needed for phonographic cylinders. After a year of the empirical trials Edison had urged upon him he was ready to admit defeat and quit. "Then it came like a flash of lightning. Not the Edison way." When asked by Edison how he got the wax, Rosanoff replied triumphantly, "I got it with theo-retical chemistry. It took exactly fifteen minutes to get it!"

We may sympathize with critics like Rickover and Conant who seek to turn the schools from the nihilistic view of an education as a progression through a vista of specific trainings. Their backward glance at formal discipline, however, offers no better prospect. Whenever tests have been made with experimental controls, formal discipline has lost the day. One can depend on no automatic transfer from "hard" subjects, demanding curricula, or stern discipline. Even when regarded as only a tool, mathematics does not necessarily transfer, as has been mentioned already in the discussion of prerequisites. Even if we agree with Judd (1936) that mathematics and language are the transfer subjects par excellence, he and his students were able to make them transfer only under carefully developed conditions, and not always with certainty. Apparently, reforms without theory (empirical) or with inadequate theory (formal discipline) have both been unsuccessful in education. A theory is needed which will make more probable *how* to teach (and learn) for transfer and for the capacity to find new alternatives.

II PERCEPTUAL BASIS OF AFTER-LEARNING

*. . . . a significant idea of organization cannot be
obtained in a world in which everything is
necessary and nothing is contingent.*

N. Wiener

We start with the observation that the newborn is not a *tabula
rasa* but rather a complex system of ongoing activity. While
chemical energies of oxygen and foods must be extracted from the
environment to maintain the basic metabolism of the organism,
quite as important is the information from the structures of other
environmental energies indicating dangers, sources of food and
water, and whatever else meets its needs.

In the past, stimulation was thought of almost exclusively in
terms of external energies assaulting the organism. This caused
many observers to miss the active dynamic demand and selectivity
of these energies by the organism. A neglect of how the learner
perceives the learning task has led to fundamental errors in formulations about learning and transfer. Information from the external
environment is always received and interpreted by the organism's
frame of reference. One is reminded of the Japanese, who no
matter how much they borrowed from the Chinese and now the
Western, particularly American, cultures have always put their
distinctive stamp on everything they adopted, whether it was Bud-
dhism or a pinball machine.

Immersed in a world of different kinds of radiant, mechanical,
and chemical energies, the organism possesses sense organs capa-

14

ble of being affected by only a small proportion of them. But even with a sense organ, the probability of being stimulated depends on the threshold, intimately tied to the needs of the organism at the moment and the direction of attention. A sound may be subliminal for a distracted subject but liminal when he attends to the same sound. Also notable are the unrealized potential stimuli beyond the limited span of attention.

The energy changes in the environment remain only potential stimuli until their intensity or extent are enough to discharge a sense organ and to be discriminated at some level. A subliminal visual stimulus that remains at a constant low intensity can be summated by repetitions to become liminal (Haslerud, 1959). Gaito (1964) proposed an interesting theory of how information can range from an unconscious state, through partial information, to complete information that is entirely conscious. The progression shows up in the repeated tachistoscopic presentation of an unknown stimulus, e.g., the nonsense syllable ZIT.

Johdai (1956) contended that most learning situations are so arranged that changes of perception cannot be differentiated easily in behavior. However, in a Dashiell-type stylus maze he showed how suddenly even a long-reinforced path can suffer extinction when the direction of a psychological force changes with one or two trials of nonreinforcement. Similarly in an experiment of mine, the established pattern of turns in preceding free units changed rapidly when subsequent prescribed goal units had the accustomed paths made culs-de-sac. Analogous mechanical guidance left the free unit turns unaltered, as though changes at the goal had not been perceived (Haslerud, 1953).

With his demonstration of the intimate relation between the feedback loop (reafference) and self-initiated movements, Held (1965) showed that a one-way conception of sensory adjustment to prisms was untenable. Likewise, not until he changed from the conventional perspective did Teuber (1964) find a solution to "the riddle of the frontal lobes." "I now believe," he said, "that analysis of frontal lobe functions requires that we begin from that end, considering how these anterior parts act upon posterior, and predominantly sensory structures." My perceptual theory, starting with the organism's needs in the Theater of Perception and their interaction with the returning input of information of the cybernetic loop, also has advantages over past unidirectional theories.

Figure 1 portrays the organism as an amoeba-like construct with an active integrative center, the Theater of Perception,* from which go inquiries for information into the environmental energies without and into the Apperceptive Mass within. The latter is depicted in an evenly spaced density of dots to contrast its unconsciousness with the white of the conscious Theater of Perception and with the irregular netting of the neutral environment. The small circle in Figure 1 may remind some of a synapse, but it is intended as only a focus on a bit of relational information for the outgoing (solid) arrow and the origin for the incoming (dotted) feedback arrow. Attention as the most active region of the Theater of Perception swells momentarily the boundaries of immediate apprehension as it focuses here and there. The organism's condition determines the stimulation; only what the organism is ready for will become information.

Admittedly, the environment may present problems for the organism, e.g., too much heat. To solve such a problem a simple unconscious reflex sweating reaction may occur, but there may also be a visual survey of the surroundings to locate a shady place.

The organism has physiological needs for maintenance, growth, and defense. These affect the information gathering of the organism by lowering the threshold for stimuli related to the particular needs. The limen for danger and defense seldom rises above the availability level and therefore is nearly always ready immediately. The sensitivity to a hot surface remains close to the receptive level, but the satiated organism no longer notices signs of food. For most situations, however, the typical state is a relatively high limen which can only be lowered temporarily, followed by a resumption

* The Theater of Perception gives no plays and has no actors. It is just the place where the action is, or as Webster puts it, "A place of enactment of significant events or action."

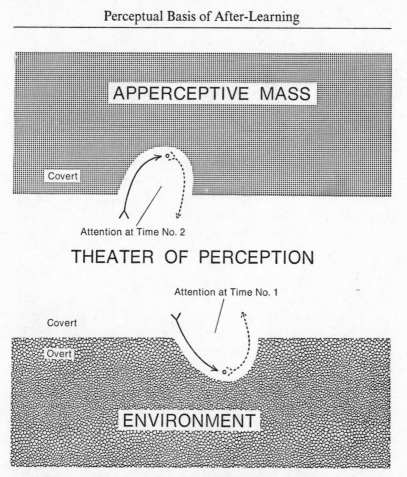

Figure 1. Attention focused into the neutral environment and the unconscious Apperceptive Mass from the Theater of Perception with its various degrees of consciousness.

of a high limen when the organism has moved its attention to another matter.

Fatigue, distractibility, and continuous demands of life end one perceptual process and inevitably cause a shift to another more urgent. Little or no perseveration can be observed. When one process ends, its threshold snaps back to a high level as though it had been a spring under tension.

The organism may always be ready for certain stimuli, e.g., loud

17

sounds, sudden changes, etc. The threshold for these are so low that special training is necessary to prevent them from interfering with all other stimuli. With them there is a short circuiting of the warm-up and repetition processes, which are usually needed for less powerful stimuli.

With stimuli for which there is no native readiness, to get a low enough threshold for immediate response requires an antecedent preparation. For highly charged or traumatic emotional situations one trial or experience may be enough: A person does not have to be nearly drowned twice to be afraid of water. One- or few-trial learning can also be observed where the stimulus is simple to discriminate and where the whole learning process has been effectively isolated from all distractions. For later eliciting of response by such a special situation one may need a preparatory warm-up period as well as a maintenance of the control of distractions. With less controlled situations, difficultly discriminated stimuli, and more complex situations, many trials may be necessary to learn (prepare) a low threshold for future crossing. Learning accentuates the discriminatory process and lowers thresholds just as attention does.

Two problems come to mind. First, can the evocation by a stimulus after a period of time be regarded as just a perseveration of the original lowering of threshold? And second, why is the response not immediately forthcoming when the given stimulus which had been learned is presented?

Organisms under certain situations may repeat a pattern, but there is little perseveration despite neural reverberations and the redundancy in stimulation. Basically this is because the stimulus ceases to be functional with more than a few seconds of focusing. The active organism moves on and attends toward new stimuli. Consequently, after a period of time one needs a new evocation and the promptness will depend on how much preparation is again necessary to lower the threshold sufficiently for the special stimulus. Between the original learning and the revival the stimulus threshold for the response remains high and unconscious.

The second problem of availability is one of getting the discriminatory processes active enough to locate the stimulus appropriate for the threshold prepared by earlier learning. Out of the multitude of energies surrounding the individual the problem is to focus upon that which can evoke the learned available reaction. Like a radar scanner the discriminatory process narrows its oscillations.

What is focused upon is limited, both in number and sequentiality. For the very small child the amount discriminable may be only a single object. With growth, the amount increases until in the adult we find for many kinds of materials the limit 7 ± 2 (Miller, 1956). Similarly, the temporal succession of items must occur within a rather narrow time span, shorter for the child than for the adult.

The memory span, or span of attention as it is also called, can be widened by some kind of organization, coding, categorization, grouping, accent, or meaning. While the absolute number of letters may be four or five times as great, the span for discrete words has about the same limit as for discrete letters. The units are larger "chunks," to use Miller's language.

Context must be recognized as the essential frame for every perceptual process (Street, 1931). A stimulus change becomes apparent as a difference with respect to the ground. If the same intensity of the stimulus is maintained but a modification is made in the ground, the same difference would be reported as though the stimulus figure had been changed. Simultaneous and successive contrasts, similarly, exhibit mutual interaction as figure and ground. Moreover, sense organs and perceptual processes alike develop an adaptation level which acts much like any other context.

Both the externally produced and internally produced stimuli are immediately perceived as information or meaning. As J. J. Gibson (1966) has pointed out, perceptions require no special transmutation by the sense organs. The meaning may be ambiguous at first and may need repeated feedback probings to settle finally upon a stable fact about the environment. The completed perceptual process moves to an idiomotor response. A person searching his memory or a handy calendar for the date to put on the check he is writing may observe narrowing approximations of his perceptions which finally result in the writing of the date on the check.

When Tinker and Goodenough (1931) studied the changes in perception of four subjects who read in a mirror meaningful books ten minutes a day for almost half a year, they found a gradual improvement in speed and accuracy due to "identifying words upon the basis of a smaller number of determining elements" rather than upon context which was the main resource at first. Apparently mirror reversal learning, as also in the Stratton-type of experiment, involves only partial new unlearning and learning because perception of many of the relations remains essentially similar to the normal situation.

Postman and Bruner (1951) showed how context "rectified" the reversal of one letter in meaningful words exposed tachistoscopically, but its absence from meaningless groups of letters led to much easier detection of a change. Tinker and Goodenough found that their subjects, especially the rapid readers, were so affected by the strong context of their material that on unclear words they were apt to substitute a synonym so as not to change the context.

For a situation which includes no more discrete elements than one's span of attention an immediate, accurate response can be emitted. That limit defines the span. Wickelgren (1965) believes that immediate memory perseverates acoustically. Whether something analogous occurs visually, or whether the visual span is also acoustically mediated, is interesting to conjecture.

Return now to Figure 1. The covert unconscious world can provide information from past learning and from unlearned readinesses of the nervous or humoral systems. The spotlight of attention can focus on the cybernetic circuits in and out of the Apperceptive Mass, much as on those dealing with environmental energies. While attention focuses at one point, only marginal attention can be elsewhere, e.g., focusing attention on a search in the Apperceptive Mass will perforce raise the threshold for stimuli from the environmental energies (Webster and Haslerud, 1964). Whatever is attended to may become dazzlingly conscious, contrasting with a penumbra fading into unconsciousness. It also dominates for a moment the feedback to the sense organs and related muscles to maximize by orientation the information-securing possibilities.

Since the Theater of Perception acts only in the "specious present," as James called it, Table 1 outlines its temporal boundaries and suggests the way it apprehends the perceptual past and future. By special processes discussed in chapter IV immediate memory can become part of the longtime store of the Apperceptive Mass and later can be retrieved from the memory to bring formerly processed information to the service of present needs in the Theater of Perception. Similarly, the future can become equally available by devices examined in chapter VII. Thus man's potentiality for living in three worlds complicates his life but also makes possible his freedom and self-control.

Table 1 portrays a flow chart centering in the Theater of Perception. It makes explicit the parallel communication loops between the Theater of Perception and the external world on the one side and the Apperceptive Mass on the other. Both sides provide information through stimuli which may be defined as changes in the quantity and configuration of energies. The frame of reference is the adaptation level of a physiological zero or the comparable perceptual habituation level (Helson, 1964). Learning or special attention can change limens of sensitivity at parts of the adaptation level barrier, and thus provide for differential receptiveness for a certain strength of stimulus. For example, the person who has studied a little botanical taxonomy notices more differences in leaves and bark on varieties of oaks than on those he had formerly classified only as trees. On the covert side, cues to initiate retrieval sets into the Apperceptive Mass serve a similar filtering function.

For J. J. Gibson (1966) the environment has a structure of which the edges, gradients, and other areas of change can provide information. The perceptual systems discriminate the invariants in a changing environmental world to stabilize what might otherwise be a welter of contrary stimulation. The Apperceptive Mass has analogous information at nodes of the feedback loops.

The cybernetic loops returning information to the Theater of

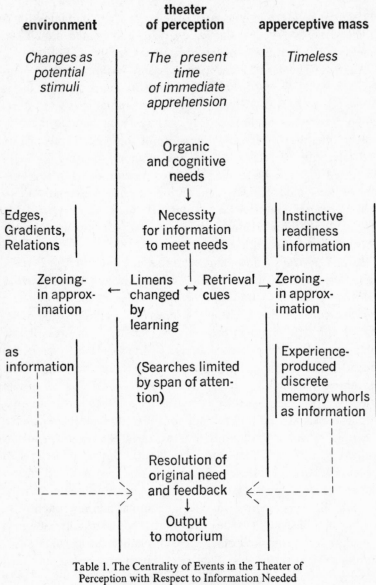

Table 1. The Centrality of Events in the Theater of
Perception with Respect to Information Needed
from the Environment and the
Apperceptive Mass

Perception have a direct effect on the activity there. However, the function within the Theater may be influenced indirectly through feedback from a prior idiomotor response. This could be from kinesthetic feedback or by restimulation of the organism by overt changes made in the environment by the response. Within the covert world of Apperceptive Mass and Theater of Perception similar feedback may occur.

The similarities in perceptual processes interacting with the external and internal worlds may remind some people of the Gestaltist's isomorphism. However, that term referred to correlated outer and inner relations of the forms found in the world. The brain fields, Köhler contended, do not copy the phenomenal world but have equivalent relationships. In the present theory it is not the world that is dynamically re-created internally but a method of getting information which uses similar feedback loops toward both the Apperceptive Mass and the external world. These processes develop ontogenetically, probably mostly by learning, but phylogenetic development might also be investigated. Obviously my postulations about information as searched from and processed in the Theater of Perception have no resemblance to the isomorphism of the Gestaltists.

III IMMEDIATE APPREHENSION IMMEDIATE MEMORY

*All nature is to be found
in the smallest things.*
Latin proverb

Those like Melton (1963) who see immediate memory and longtime memory as a continuum with the number of cues necessary for retrieval the only variable neglect the qualitative differences in a here-and-now existence. As far as can be inferred by the behavior of animals, this is the kind of world they live in (except possibly those animals brought into a world of time by specific conditioning with temporal intervals as an additional variable, i.e., in Pavlov's trace experiments). This here-and-now world is also the one most humans live in the majority of their waking hours.

Consider the simple problem of dialing or telling an operator a number one is telephoning for the first time. The company has to take into consideration the limited span of attention and memory. For calls in a local exchange, where most calls are made, the number of digits is only four or five, well below the adult span and within the span of the elementary school child. For numbers beyond the local exchange, inclusion of the exchange number and area code quickly gets beyond the average person's span. The telephone company has an educational campaign to encourage people to write such new numbers before dialing to reduce the problem of wrong numbers. Typically for a local number you

24

expect to call only once you remember it long enough to dial, but if a busy signal means a delay and need for redialing, many people will find it necessary to look up the number again.

The here-and-now situation, severely bounded by attention to a limited group of stimuli on the one side, has a wall of undelayed response on the other. If response must be delayed, then special retrieval cues must be found—like writing down the telephone number or noting some of its distinctive sequences, e.g., 2-4-6-8. Attention too may be distracted by other more pressing needs of the active organism, e.g., to find out who is knocking at the front door.

Problem solving in the here-and-now world is largely restricted to the serious business of immediate needs. The organism must get information on what will make the satisfaction possible. For the young animal, phylogenetic selection provides hereditarily when in a condition of need, e.g., hunger, for a very low threshold for certain environmental energies that can act as releasers of an adjustive act (Tinbergen, 1951). Baby birds arouse themselves and stick up their necks when the nest wall shakes slightly on the arrival of the parent with food. The baby birds will exhibit the same reaction if an experimenter lightly taps the edge of the nest.

Out of the endless number of impinging energies only those few that the organism is ready for will affect sense organs and set off a neural afferent, informative message to the Theater of Perception. First the potential stimulus must be changing in order to be detected, and then the organism must identify (discriminate) whether it is the information needed. For the simplest animals, e.g., Tinbergen's young birds, detection and identification may be commingled. For the more complex, the detection may be the "What is it?" unlearned reflex Pavlov noticed in his dogs or the startle reaction if the stimulus has unusual intensity. Then the identification depends on the discriminable cues. For many situations all such energies are as available as the readiness of the organism permits.

The number of discrete items the organism can attend to with a single impression, the span, starts with one for the very young child but increases approximately by one for each year's maturation during the preschool period to five and then more gradually until the adult level 7 ± 2 (Miller, 1956) is reached at the beginning of adolescence.

What is included in a discrete visual or auditory item changes also with maturation and experience. According to Bartlett (1932), some schema which does not increase the number of discrete items but changes them would be like the date "1776" instead of a "1" followed by a "7" followed by another "7" and then a "6." Examples of innate categorization can be found in Tinbergen's experiments where an airplane-like cutout approaching birds with one angle of wings was reacted to with fear, as if the model were a hawk, whereas when the cutout was turned around so that the wings were at a different angle, the reaction was one of indifference.

Kolers (1966) made an interesting contribution to the question of the integration within immediate memory. He determined whether $n/2$ input of information for each of two languages was responded to as $n/2$ or n input of information from a single language. The results indicated that the probability of recall of unconnected words increases with the frequency of occurrence, regardless of the difference between input from two languages or one. Quite apart from the implication of Kolers's study for semantics, it offers a valuable heuristic model of the way information from various sources accrues and integrates in the Theater of Perception.

The time within which the human adult organism can survey and identify the information in immediate apprehension lasts no more than a few seconds, which is ample for the solving of elementary human problems. The simple but adequate measurement of this period by Peterson and Peterson (1959) showed that the person recalling a single trigram, e.g., XMC, cannot resist the distraction of subtracting successive 3's from a given number. Within three seconds he could remember it only half the time, by nine seconds only a quarter of the time, and by eighteen seconds for all practical purposes the trigram was irretrievable. Likewise, Broadbent emphasized the selectivity of the filters for incoming information and suggested the principle that attention favors orientation to novel messages. He postulated fast decay of information in immediate memory, i.e., any interruption will cause its disappearance (Broadbent, 1963). However, Crossman (1967), by asking for information at various times after exposure, found evidence of some temporary storage because material could be reexamined by attending to it. On the basis of his results he proposed a unidirectional perceptual process with temporary restraining baffles at points along the way and with additional information on pattern elements and complex patterns coming from two permanent stores. In my perceptual theory the Theater of Perception provides for the temporary storage processes found in Crossman's system, but the Apperceptive Mass differs greatly from his permanent storage, both in what is stored and how it is retrieved.

With young children and perhaps some animals eidetic imagery, i.e., photographic memory, prolongs the period within which information can be maintained for immediate apprehension in the Theater of Perception. G. W. Allport (1924) considered this valuable for survival, especially if lacking experience. Even in the adult visual stimulation is followed by positive and then by negative afterimages which can be prolonged for experimental study by special techniques. For eidetic imagery in the young child the mechanism is still unknown. The tendency gradually diminishes to practically a zero level in adulthood. Haber and Haber (1964) found only 8 per cent of elementary school children meeting a strict criterion for eidetic imagery. School age children, especially in the United States where extra stimulation may force precocious development, are probably too old for such a study. Haber discovered that the use of eidetic ability on a particular situation did not enhance memory retrieval of the occasion any better than for noneidetic occasions. With eidetic imagery, however, the young child can review and impress the scene and even observe and manipulate the movement of individuals within it (Klüver, 1926).

Figure 2 shows a continuous line arrow leaving the need for information and going to a small, unfilled circle, symbolizing some approximating focus on a figure against the general ground of the environment. That informatory relation is then the beginning of a dotted arrow back to the Theater of Perception. When the ultimate information, symbolized by a large filled circle, has been reached, the dotted feedback arrow then goes to an interaction with the original need instead of starting another approximating cycle. The figures in the environmental ground correspond to the nodes shown in the Apperceptive Mass of subsequent graphs. At first the search includes as wide a span of attention as the organism allows. The approximating loops concentrate attention as the discriminating process continues. When this reaches a critical level, the integration with other input will finally dispatch to the motorium for response.

Wertheimer and the other Gestaltists showed by ingenious demonstrations and experiments that the environmental energies have such order and relationships that their information can be apprehended immediately by an alert organism. Proximity, similarity, closure, and good continuation all tend in the direction of "good" and stable forms and patterns. The stars appear grouped in constellations, although some primitive men saw a great bear where

THEATER OF PERCEPTION

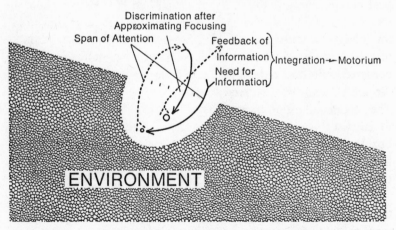

Figure 2. Immediate memory in the Theater of Perception of information discriminated among environmental energies.

we now see a dipper. Koffka (1935) postulated that dynamic closure makes complete forms like a triangle out of three dots not in a straight line. J. J. Gibson (1966) sought experimentally to find what minimal invariant relationships are necessary to provide information of triangularity. Picasso (1947) explained how "a picture used to be a sum of additions. In my case a picture is a sum of destructions. . . . In the end, though, nothing is lost." To illustrate he made a series of lithographs of a bull. Starting with a literal representation, he subtracted repeatedly until he ended with an abstract line drawing which unmistakably is a bull. As he said, ". . . basically a picture doesn't change, [for] the first 'vision' remains almost intact, in spite of appearances. . . ."

The Gestaltists would probably contend that Picasso had intuitively and experimentally discovered the essential form of "bullishness." Eleanor Gibson (1969) would ask what perceptual learning of such invariants had occurred in both the artist and the viewer to make Picasso's communication intelligible.

While the Köhler insight experiments are usually described as dealing with learning and various psychologists have attempted to incorporate them into trial-and-error formulations as just a faster variety (Mowrer, 1960), they are also examples of the creative possibilities in immediate apprehension. Köhler's chimpanzees seemed incapable of retrieving from memory what was essential for solving the problem, even though it was a means, e.g., a box, that had been shown to them in the next room. The solutions occurred only with means that could be perceived together with the goal. The insight consisted essentially in a new relationship. The chimpanzee, after exhausting direct trial-and-error approaches to the goal, would change his position. This at times brought the box and the goal of suspended fruit together in the same visual field, a favorable condition for perceiving the box as a means to the goal.

Archery, like other motor skills, has often been taught by having the learner practice regularly, get knowledge of results from his score at the target, and receive suggestions from his teacher about correction of position, timing, and other mistakes. The entirely different approach of Zen in Japan has been described by Herrigl (1953). Instead of daily practice in dispatching the arrow, the Zen master had his pupil, Herrigl, develop a new perception of himself, the bow, the arrow, and the bull's-eye. For months the master would not let him release the bow. Finally when the man, the arrow, and the target had been unified, the arrow sped to the middle of the bull's-eye. While the Western man may express skepticism about a result obtained with such neglect of all he believes about the value of practice and correction of technique, Eastern wisdom may have many valuable lessons on the basic invariants, to use J. J. Gibson's term. In Zen these are conveyed indirectly through analogies, stories, and the perceptual leap required to get out of the encircling walls of the paradox. The late Dr. Koji Sato for more than a decade scattered articles on many of these among the experimental reports in his *Psychologia*, a feedback journal from the East to the West.

IV RETRIEVAL

> . . . *the readiness is all.*
>
> Shakespeare

When the recall response is delayed more than a few seconds after stimulation, the behavior must be reinitiated with retrieval cues. These are given this name because some reduction in randomness of the organism's contribution to interaction in the Theater of Perception takes place during original learning. When the retrieval cue occurs later, a resemblance to the original perception has been made somewhat probable.

Ebbinghaus's savings method (relearning to the same criterion used on the original learning) is a good prototype of the retrieval process. The original number of trials or time measures the effort to perceive discriminatively the items in a list of nonsense syllables well enough to set up efficient feedback loops. On relearning, the syllables reach criterion according to the amount of interfering intrusions and reorganizations that have occurred with some or all of the materials since original learning. This problem of retroactive inhibition is the familiar one of new experiences overlaying and confusing old ones. For example, the twelve trials necessary to repeat once a list of ten nonsense syllables correctly may require fifteen trials of relearning if a very similar list has been learned in the meantime.

In rote learning of a list one builds an interconnected group of

31

responses by the intent-to-recall the next item from the cue of the previous one. As Thorndike had found, a person might have difficulty recalling what item preceded a certain one but could, when he had met the criterion, tell easily what followed it. The perception of relationship is often directional. Unless earlier learning had reached a high degree of discrimination of cues for each successive pair in the chain, subsequent interpolated learning could easily divert and confuse the original directionality.

A hungry rat is trained to cross a space for food located behind the one lighted door among three. When the light cue is removed before the rat is released, the problem becomes insoluble even for a rat with body orientation if the delay lasts more than a few seconds. However, if the space traversed is lengthened to compensate for the time needed to reach the doors and the light cue is extinguished only when the rat is in motion, the delay may go as high as 11 1/2 seconds (McAllister, 1932). With a different, more direct technique of jumping from a central point to four alternatives at 90° separations, MacCorquodale (1947) found that eleven rats could delay up to ten minutes. Responses following one-minute delays were above chance even after such disturbances to orientation as rotating the jumping platform or shifting doors during the delay.

Apparently, the rat with excellent learning abilities for fixed cue situations has a very limited capacity to respond to contingencies with a hiatus. This inability contrasts markedly with delays in the rhesus monkeys. When food is put under one of several objects and then an opaque screen is lowered to separate the objects and the monkey for as much as thirty seconds, the normal animal has no trouble picking the object covering the food. Whereas the rats can only maintain a rigid stance or be oriented and placed in motion toward the object (McAllister, 1932), the monkey may dance around his cage while waiting for the opaque door to be raised (Jacobson and Haslerud, 1935). Delays of several days are possible in higher animals like the chimpanzee and the gorilla (Yerkes, 1928). Man can succeed with even longer delays in a similar situation if some words like "middle one" can be used.

Since the chimpanzee and the monkey lack this auditory symbolic response to mediate the delay, one must postulate in their complex nervous system some persisting feedback loops or some discriminating perceptions which allow an easy reinitiation of behavior. The evidence is against perseveration beyond a few seconds (Peterson and Peterson, 1959); the hypothesis of perceptual discrimination of variable contingencies seems more credible. How the organism stores the information neurologically is not yet known, but this does not concern us here since we shall be dealing only with constructs.

When a person says on changing an activity, "Now to put on a different hat," he recognizes how important his set is. If one has been thinking and doing subtraction, some errors may occur when one begins to add, as happens while keeping a checkbook straight. A change in set can remove much of the interference in a retroactive recall, even when the interpolation timing and material would make one predict a good deal of retroactive inhibition (Postman and Postman, 1948).

The present theory supposes that retrieval cues operate only from the Theater of Perception. The retrieval cue is a word, image, or other factor that can begin an afferent, tentative loop toward the high threshold intents-to-recall in the Apperceptive Mass. The returning side of the loop then lowers the threshold, claims temporarily a more central place in attention and, with the perceptual process now active, a corrective approximation on the ensuing loops. The organization of original intents and of retrieval cues makes it possible to drive toward even narrower and more exact associations.

The successive discriminations in a retrieval search can be conceived of as centripetal. It is really a set or dynamic tendency to zero in on the literal, previous learned objective. Without the set or tension, organization by itself is insufficient. The Apperceptive Mass can be conceived of as consisting of *independent* centripetal whorls whose functional connection can be made only to the Theater of Perception. Any organization in a group of whorls

33

would entail a succession of or simultaneous group of retrieval cues, spreading like a fan from the Theater of Perception.

Retrieval cues as behavior supports guide or set limits to the excursions of the feedback loops (Haslerud, 1957). A continuity of relations between the Theater of Perception and the Apperceptive Mass always exists, but to segregate and lower the threshold for easy perception of the relations needs attention and restrictions. Physiologically the correlation may be the ordering of brainwaves, e.g., the replacement of the alpha rhythm by the faster beta waves in a subject attending to a new problem.

From Kurt Lewin's laboratory in Berlin the Zeigarnik effect added dynamic tension for retrieval to the Ebbinghaus prototype (Zeigarnik, 1938). Similar to the Zeigarnik effect was an old study done by J. Peterson in 1916. By contrasting how much simple recall recovered with a "determination to recall," especially after a 48-hour period, he showed that an intent-to-recall has an effect. When warned that they would be asked to reproduce the list, his subjects attempted by grouping, associating with mental images, or making sentences out of the words to hold the list, and they did approximately 50 per cent better with determination. The interruption of an ongoing activity will increase not only the probability of resuming an ego-involved, interesting activity, but also the recall of the list of still incomplete activities. The two kinds of retrieval, in speech and in motor response, both testify to the presence of some kind of tension or, as used in this book, of an intent-to-recall. This becomes the response evoked later by the cue of the retrieval set.

Civilized man has tremendous aids to retrieval in his social inheritance of language and books. Yet, even primitive man did not have to learn and recall as a lone individual. Because of the overlap of the generations, and because of long early dependency, the child could tap the memories and the habit systems of the elders. Within similar limits this has been observed in the chimpanzee and even in the Japanese monkey (Imanishi, 1957; Frisch, 1959).

Man's culture has been cumulative because of the possibility of social retrieval. The elders may know how to perform a certain task, e.g., how to build a house, and may be willing to teach or permit imitation. The basic stimulus in social transmission is an indication of the place to work on a problem. This may be supplemented by social information about specific means, e.g., how to make the corners of the house square.

As Miller and Dollard (1941) proved, the white rat can be conditioned to respond to the cues provided by the activity of another rat that had learned a maze. To make use of the social retrieval resources the one who imitates must already have the basic skills or elements which the skilled act puts into a new configuration or perspective (Hayes and Hayes, 1967). The child must be able to read before he can get information from books. Until the young chimpanzee has matured enough and has developed elementary skills of perceiving and acting, it is unable to retrieve from the group's collective learning (Birch, 1945; Schiller, 1952).

From the second month when the social smile appears, the presence and activities of people stimulate a child more than anything else with the exception of the most violent situations. The helplessness and dependence of the child make the example of those dominant in his life the most compelling stimulation. This obviously influences elementary learning and allows the child to start at a more sophisticated level than he could without such aid. Eventually the accumulated experience of the parents is supplemented by the total social resources of the group, and the individual may seek out and elicit knowledge from many sources.

What will be retrieved from social resources depends on how open the person is to such stimulation. For example, a library might as well not exist for those who never use it. Moreover, the social memory there may fail to disclose its information unless one has learned to think like a cataloger and to categorize like the author of reference books. Social imitation also seems related to hierarchy, at least in chimpanzees. A dominant male does not learn a skill like opening a coconut from a female who knows the trick, and among the females those higher in dominance do not learn from those lower (Elder, 1961 personal communication).

Among Japanese monkeys, however, Imanishi (1957) reported that new foods were first eaten by the young and that the mothers then learned from their children. Tolman (1932) emphasized "docility" as a necessary condition for perceptual learning. Just as hubris has been called the great sin by religious writers, something similar may represent a limitation on retrieval of social knowledge. Only recently have doctors in Western Europe and the New World reexamined the devices and methods of the witch doctors of Africa, of the practitioners of acupuncture in old Chinese medicine, and of the *curanderos* of South America. Scattered in the superstition are golden nuggets of valuable drugs and insights into psychotherapy (Seguín, 1968; Sato, 1957).

Civilized man has formalized in educational systems the preparation of the child to retrieve from the social store. It is surprising how often the essential psychological conditions for attaining that goal have been left out of consideration. Many times it is by happy accident rather than by design that an adolescent continues eagerly to learn from his elders personally or through books. A sad commentary on educational efforts even in universities is the smallness of the minority who continue to learn after graduation.

In addition to a positive reinforcement of reading and a respect for the source that can be discriminated as more expert than another, the child needs to learn how to gain access to the materials worth retrieving. One can see that in a world where society is accumulating printed material faster than ever before so that libraries are filled almost before any new additions are completed the individual must become an expert in using reference materials. The civilized man owes an increasing debt to those who catalog the books and make the card indices, those who collect, abstract, and index the increasing literature in each field of knowledge, the makers of dictionaries and encyclopedias, and those who devise ways to use computers for retrieval systems. Although few situations warrant learning and remembering much specific information, certainly among that little there ought to be retrieval cues for searching library sources.

The modern school that makes a "resource center" the very

heart of the educational process allows the child to see very early how he can amplify his personal resources and experiences by learning how to draw on the vast social reservoir. The emphasis then shifts from training the individual to remember well to training him how to retrieve and as importantly, how to discriminate the relative value of what is thus made available. Formerly the person with a good memory, like the law-sayers of Iceland a thousand years ago who recited the accumulated laws as the people assembled on summer days at Thyngvallir, was highly valued. Now with our modern flood of knowledge the discriminative, expert retriever obviously serves both himself and others more functionally than does the individual with the flawless memory.

Before we proceed to examine the nature of the retrieval cue and to propose a paradigm, we ought to consider the problems of incidental learning and of interference in learning. How relatively available are associations developed in the neighborhood of a specific learning? Although the small child's eidetic imagery allows him to report on aspects of a picture not specifically attended to or required on initial presentation and disappears as the child grows toward maturity, a more general capacity for incidental learning continues (Klüver, 1926). When Japanese and American school children were compared, the Japanese, reading from the top to the bottom of a column of print, perceived incidentally what was above the point of focus; the American children, reading from left to right, perceived incidentally to the left of the focus of the material to be specifically learned (Haslerud and Motoyoshi, 1961). Another kind of directionality in learning and retrieval has been extensively studied in Japan. Umemoto (1959) reviewed his own and others' experiments on the Kuraishi phenomenon. Beginning with observations supported by measurements of reaction time and errors for the greater ease of translating from a foreign language into one's own than vice versa, the studies have extended to more general paired associates in a free recall situation. Response items are favored in recall over those on the stimulus side, except when the responses are more difficult, e.g., nonsense syllables, as compared with easy stimulus items like letters of the alphabet.

Incidental learning and its retrieval have been less studied than intentional learning despite the fact that most of what a person knows has not been deliberately learned. Because the cues of incidental learning are situational rather than specific, an attempt to retrieve some of its aspects may have to depend on interpolation from a rather global association or feeling.

Interferences create a problem in retrieval, ranging from the "tip of the tongue" phenomenon to complete amnesia. The competing responses, as diagrammed in Figure 6, develop where similar situations have been insufficiently discriminated. Since retrieval involves a step-by-step approximation and a closing in on the learned item, any distracting association or emotional tension may divert or block the activity of the retrieval cue. But the common, undramatic sequence of one learning after another has an equally strong effect on retrieval as exhibited in proactive and retroactive inhibition, the interfering effect of similar learning that follows too closely the end of the original learning. This is particularly true when the original and interpolating learnings are not well organized or meaningful as in the case of one list of nonsense syllables being followed by another list. To develop and maintain a functional retrieval cue one must therefore see that inhibiting factors are controlled and try to facilitate the desired cues.

Recognition with its additional cues produces more correct identifications than does non-cued recall. Tulving and Pearlstone (1966) interpret the way category names aid recall as evidence of different levels of accessibility. Some kinds of information are apparently inaccessible under ordinary conditions of recall. Although Saugstad and Raaheim (1960) contend that the information to solve a problem will occur if the subject has it available, the experience may have left traces in storage but still be unobtainable according to Tulving.

One may now wonder what a retrieval cue is. One should remember that after a delay the situation has to be reconstructed. When a child asks where the light has gone when the electric light switch is turned off, one can only explain that no light exists except when the filament is heated. The retrieval cue then can be only an initiator of the process of recall, or of resurgence of the intent-to-recall. The cue for the retrieval set may be a word, a question (e.g., "How many days has September?"), an image of the person's face whose name one wants to remember, a feeling of contentment, or a wish to recollect a particular event. When the recall occasion arrives, the cue initiates a process similar to that introduced during the learning.

Since most situations have not been overlearned to the point of complete isolation, the retrieval cue initiates a searching sort of set with a centripetal direction. Each feedback permits the situation to be reperceived and a closer approximation to be attempted. A question, "Who was president of the United States in 1941?" starts a recruitment of additional cues that are in the approximate locale of the answer, e.g., "When was World War II?" "When did Roosevelt's long term of office end?" If a person had learned isolated items by rote, information in the "locale" would be meaningless and unserviceable for him. Missing the response because the exact conditioned stimulus had not been given, he could not search for the desired response because a retrieval set had not been part of that restricted learning.

The savings method employs the least common denominator of retrieval cues. The retrieval set in this case is instigated by the instructions in the original learning to anticipate the next syllable in the list from stimulation by the preceding syllable.

A more usual memorial situation develops the retrieval set as a completion or closure. When the response fails, the prompter in the wings whispers the next cue to the actor. When no handy prompter exists, a retrace to a well-rehearsed part or a leap forward to the next familiar place may locate some cue. Given that specific cue, the set closes onto its particular speech or episode.

Most retrieval, however, involves not the verbatim memorized speech of the actor but information flexible enough for response to many variants of a stimulating query.

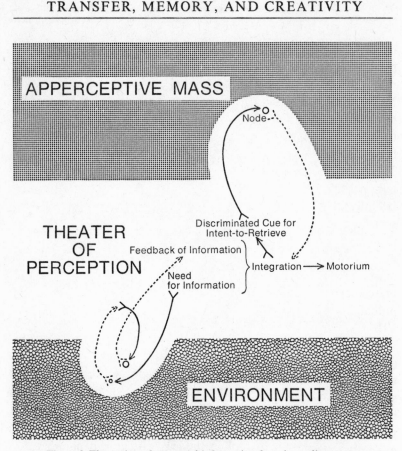

Figure 3. The saving of processed information from immediate memory by differentiating a cue for a later retrieval set to operate on the Apperceptive Mass.

During original learning the intent-to-recall ends with a very narrow ellipsoidal feedback because the object has become known. At retrieval, however, because the reconstruction proceeds by approximation, the feedback may begin almost circular and finally arrive at something like the initial narrower ellipsoid between the Apperceptive Mass and the Theater of Perception.

Figure 3 portrays how the processed information of immediate memory may be "saved" for addition to the permanent store in the Apperceptive Mass. There is a reperception (developing into an

40

intent-to-retrieve) of the information rushing toward the motorium, the attendant situation (one or more stimuli later to be the retrieval cue), and the shunt or deflection into the Apperceptive Mass (behavior feeds back on itself, its correlate being the recurrent nerves). Even though the centripetal whorl may not be carried to an explicit complete node, the set for later retrieval will have been established. The change from immediate memory in the Theater of Perception to the more permanent store is fundamentally a shift from the automatic to the at least partly conscious intentional. In the rat this set can be carried by anticipating the specific goal (Tolman, 1932). In the mature human adult the set includes but goes beyond that to a more conscious and generalized intent to "save" or restrain what is vanishing (chapter IX). One must not think, however, that this "saving" necessarily involves prescience of a future need or use, though this greatly increases the probability of the success of the project as will be shown in chapter VII.

Every response modifies the nervous system in some respect (Hull, 1937). As Pribram (1967) has reiterated, the problem is not the getting of an impression but rather its retrieval. Some cue, some handle, must be discriminated (coded) during the fleeting immediate memory. With intense, deliberate intent-to-retrieve the vanishing immediate perception has its salient features structured or emphasized. Figure 3 portrays how this may be accomplished so that a later need for this information will find a lower threshold to initiate a reconstruction similar to the original. Any immediate perception that lacks such a distinguishing cue is like a library book mislaid before cataloging; it may still exist physically but for all practical purposes it is unavailable and a nullity. Incidental, i.e., no-intent, learning ordinarily shows that lack of retrieval control. However, if the incidental learning precedes the focusing of attention as was mentioned earlier (Haslerud and Motoyoshi, 1961), control may be under the same cue as for the focused material.

Figure 3 also has a feature that ought not to be missed—the secondary role of stimulation from the environment compared to the primary need and readiness in the Theater of Perception. Even a direct question asked from the environment cannot activate the searching processes in the Theater of Perception without the prior readiness (see Fig. 6).

Although the call on innate information in the Apperceptive Mass goes on from the beginning in the newborn, the utilization of learned memories saved there depends on an instigating retrieval cue to restart the set. In Figure 4 the need for further information than that available in the immediate environment activates the sets with lowest thresholds. Because of the groping for the most accurate expression of a memory, the retrieval set usually shows a number of centripetal approximations. A warm-up may be necessary to find the locale for proper retrieval. Sometimes this is spo-

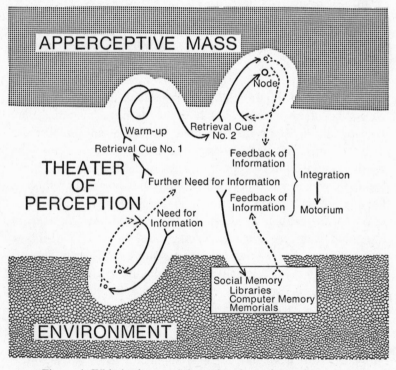

Figure 4. With inadequate information from the environment a search for further information in the Apperceptive Mass and the social memory.

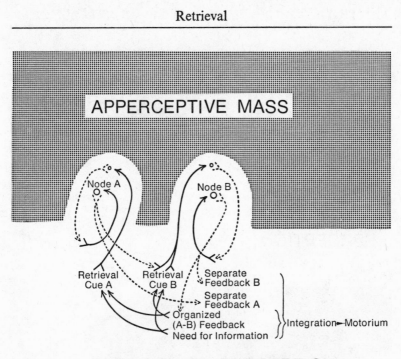

THEATER OF PERCEPTION

Figure 5. Discrete memory whorls in the Apperceptive Mass organized in the Theater of Perception.

ken of as "putting on another hat." With overlearned material the retrieved information may be indistinguishable from the original, but more often the reconstruction reveals a correction, a shift, a simplification. This indicates that the memory saved is not a thing but rather a plan or set to retrieve.

One should note in Figure 4 the store of social memory and how its feedback enters into the final interaction or resolution of information before the passage to the motorium. The cues for access to the social memory probably differ little from those directed into the Apperceptive Mass.

The perception of an organization of several bits of information is depicted in Figure 5 as an overlap in the Theater of Perception of otherwise discrete memory whorls of the Apperceptive Mass. Each may be retrieved by the specific cue for its set, but learning

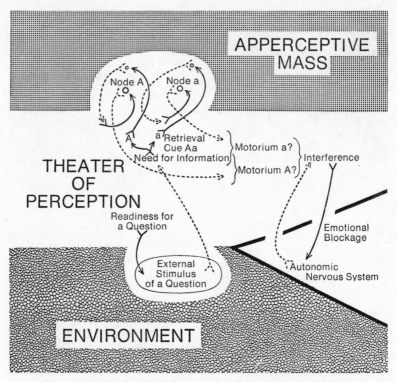

Figure 6. Retroactive inhibition by poor discrimination and unorganized learning, interference often inducing a self-perpetuating emotional circuit.

may make the feedback of one a highly probable retrieval cue for the next. Many of the gestalten of ordinary learning are probably perceived as a discrete whole and continue to function as such in a single memory whorl in the Apperceptive Mass. The theory allows for organization to arise from either planful or such accidental overlap in the Theater of Perception as in free association and incidental learning. Having the memory whorls discrete and unconscious except as they enter the Theater of Perception not only helps to integrate the phenomena of memory but, as we shall see in chapter VII, also makes possible a paradigm for getting new alternatives from old memories. Figure 5 shows too how meaning in the organized resources of the Apperceptive Mass can widen the span of attention, e.g., a group of familiar words being apprehended as accurately as a like number of discrete letters.

Figure 6 depicts inaccurate and confused recall as in retroactive inhibition. If the retrieval set was inadequately discriminated originally, e.g., *Aa* instead of *A*, *A* and *a* may each be revived with resultant confusion in the motorium. Poor organization leads to much the same result for more complex learning.

The frustration from interfering reactions may arouse the emotional system. Figure 6 illustrates how the feedback from autonomic reactions may become part of a self-perpetuating circuit instead of combining with other retrieval cues to search the Apperceptive Mass for information to solve the problem.

While Olds's memory grid implies a more specific location than that of the information nodes on cybernetic circuits between the Theater of Perception and the Apperceptive Mass, his activation of a memory address "at the same time a pattern of digit wires (carrying the code to be stored) is also activated" is like my retrieval cue and retrieval set, respectively. He further postulates that the retrieval cue's "activation of the address reactivates the digit lines and the same code which was previously stored now becomes the output" (Olds, 1969). My theory, in contrast, following Neisser (1967) rather than electronics, sees the retrieval cue as the initiator of the set which constructs anew by approximations a resemblance of the immediate perception that was "saved."

V TRANSFER

Plus ça change, plus la même
French proverb

Faculty psychology and its corollary of formal discipline reigned over the academic curriculum during the nineteenth century. To exercise a faculty would increase it and according to the pseudoscience of phrenology would even change the contour of the skull by a bulge in the area ascribed to the particular faculty. For example, the forehead above the eyes was claimed to develop as memory developed. Exponents of the classical curriculum, concerned mainly with the memorization of Greek and Latin authors, insisted that it developed memory, judgment, and many other valuable faculties (Thorndike, 1913).

The experiments of Thorndike and Woodworth (1901) tested how learning to estimate the areas of large rectangles affected the later estimation for small rectangles. They and others were surprised how little advantage (transfer) accrued from the earlier learning. Comparable experiments showed the same results.

With the demise of faculty psychology after the experiments of Thorndike and Woodworth, interest turned to ways of deriving transfer from a scientific substitute. Intuitively everyone recognized that unless the student improved during his education, the whole process of schooling would be futile. Thorndike proposed identical elements as the basis for transfer, though he recognized how seldom extensive duplication occurs. In spite of the fact that he valued even small amounts of transfer, as was mentioned in chapter I, his research continued to indicate so little transfer that he began to counsel the graduate students at Teachers College, Columbia University, to teach specifically for each situation and not to depend on transfer. The curriculum of most American schools began to change toward specificity.

What little transfer occurred was the result of the overlap in identical elements from the old to the new situation, e.g., from adding two-place numbers to adding three-place numbers. At first this suggestion applied only to the materials but later was extended to methods too; learning to be a neat writer in an English class might transfer to neatness in an arithmetic class.

Transfer following the Thorndikian restriction of proportion of identical elements was fundamentally a maintenance of the *same* reponse. Or, in other words, the problem was to see with how few common stimulus and response elements one could still get the same response as in original learning. Some critics, like Judd at the University of Chicago, suggested that it was not remarkable that Thorndike got little or no transfer—he was looking for the wrong thing and in the most unlikely place (Judd, 1908).

The Thorndikian transfer paradigm was thought by some to refer mostly to transfer by response generalization. In fact, the mirror drawing experiment to practice with one hand and to test advantage for learning with the other hand got into the experimental psychology textbooks as the typical transfer situation. Various extensions to all other prehensile members, including the mouth, were tried and showed about the same amount of transfer when the relative awkwardness or ease was equated for.

Some, like Hellebrand at the University of Wisconsin, found value in this cross education for rehabilitating those with problems of tonus and for strengthening limbs temporarily in a sling or cast (personal communication, 1960). Experimentally he found the unexercised arm gained about as much strength as the exercised one. The extension of skills from one response organ to another can be differentiated from changing responses to a maintained stimulus because it is so very much easier. In the latter case one gets interference or negative transfer.

The exhibition of the learned skill by using motor organs other than the one used in original learning, e.g., writing one's name by holding a pencil in one's toes, is really nothing new perceptually and requires just a shunt before the normal final common neural pathway.

A considerable number of studies have examined interocular transfer. In kittens, Riesen and Mellinger (1956) found that a visual discrimination habit learned monocularly could be transferred to the other eye if it had had experience with patterns but not if the only previous experience had been to diffuse light. Apparently the central neurological organization must have a background of relevant discriminatory experience.

If we now turn to the stimulus rather than the response to seek fresh alternatives, we find a long list of proponents for stimulus generalization, from Pavlov to many of today's psychologists.

Pavlov (1966) was much impressed by the phenomenon of generalization where neighboring stimuli to each side of the reinforced conditioned stimulus (e.g., to B and D when the conditioned stimulus was C on the scale) would show a gradient of responsiveness. He interpreted it as irradiation on the cortex of his canine subjects. The range was greatest when the conditioning was first established and decreased with repeated presentation of the CS and UnS. Eventually only the specific CS (e.g., tone C) and no neighboring one would bring forth the flow of saliva. The conditioned reflexes from tactile stimulation of one side of the body will occur also to tactile stimulation of corresponding places on the other side. While pursuing his companion interest in discrimination of stimuli, Pavlov discovered he could very quickly reduce the range of stimulus generalization by extinguishing the response to neighboring stimuli and at the same time continuing to reinforce the original stimulus. However, if he required too fine a discrimination or reduced the range too fast, the procedure was dangerous to the stability of the subject, for some dogs developed "experimental neuroses" and lost all conditioning.

Pavlov's concept of cortical irradiation was challenged as an explanation of the facts of generalization. Lashley and Wade (1946) and Prokasy and Hall (1963) saw the generalization as only a state of confusion and lack of discrimination. They concluded that when discrimination improved, the stimulus generalization faded away. Razran (1949) found that in language conditioning one obtained strange equivalence responses semantically, e.g., to antonyms more than to synonyms. Meaning generalized as well as clangs. The results did not accord with any simple linear irradiation.

To depend on stimulus generalization for new alternatives would be like looking to Mrs. Malaprop for wisdom. Mrs. Malaprop in Sheridan's play is continually making remarks which amuse the audience and also some of the characters in the play, e.g., speaking of her niece Lydia, she says, "She's as headstrong as an allegory on the banks of the Nile," or of Sir Anthony Absolute's son, "He is the very pineapple of politeness!" (Act III).

However, only a grammatically well-prepared individual can appreciate the humor of a malaprop. Eventually one tires of clang variations. There was no new insightful perception in Mrs. Malaprop's remarks, not nearly as much as in the child's misuse of language as he develops an understanding and control of the code of communication in his group. A four-year-old child in a sanitary household had bought a rattle for her doll. When asked why she did not give it to the doll at once, she responded, "Need to fertilize it first."

Some punsters go beyond mere clang and exhibit their wisdom by placing a problem in an unusual setting. Such a one had been repelled by the magazine *Time*'s smug, flippant complacency for many years. On finding a change in *Time* toward social concern he now calls it *About Time*. This aptness one also can see in Shakespeare's fools who often speak more wisely than their masters, e.g., Lear's fool:

Lear: Dost thou call me a fool, boy?
Fool: All thy other titles thou hast given away; that
      thou wast born with.   (Act I, sc. iv)

If the various forms of generalization seldom turn up anything new, can one expect something more from the Gestalt approach to the problem? Köhler (1947) allowed a hen to peck grain from a medium gray surface and shooed it away from a lighter one. On a test trial when the lighter background was eliminated and the food was now available also from a dark gray, the hen ate the grain from this darker gray and avoided the medium gray. He interpreted this as a relational learning of "darker than"; this transposition fitted the Gestalt theory that an organism learns relationships rather than absolute responses. Spence (1942) controverted the proposition that learning is invariably relational by demonstrating from an experiment with chimpanzees that the Köhler results can be explained by stimulus generalization. He contended that in a discrimination the direction of response is the absolute difference between the extinction generalization values subtracted from the excitatory values generated by reinforcement for the two variables compared.

Gentry, Overall, and Brown (1959) tested the Spence behavioristic resolution of the transposition problem with monkeys trained to choose the intermediate of three different sized stimuli. When they balanced absolute and relative stimulus properties during transposition testing, they found that sophisticated monkeys (with a background of various tests) responded to the "relational" factors in the situation. Inexperienced organisms may tend to respond absolutely because of restricted conditioning to one aspect of a problem.

When a problem can be presented either as a simultaneous or as a successive discrimination problem, Zeiler (1964) discovered that a number of systematic factors like time, distance of testing from training, and the amount of experience in the tasks led to stages: at first, an absolute choice; later, a gradual change to relational responses and transposition. In general, these effects were more pronounced for successive presentations.

One can agree with the Gestaltists that all learning is of relationships but still ask, "Which relationship?" "Which context?" The "darker than" relationship of Köhler's transposition experiment with the hens can be examined as a ratio just like any other Weber fraction, turning on the question of how great a difference must be present for the difference to be discriminable. Whether the training emphasizes the ratio or reinforces regularly one element of a pair, Spence (1942) perceived that differences between excitatory values from the reinforcement and inhibitory values from non-reinforcement of the other of a pair to be discriminated allowed him to predict responses for a range of changes. Beyond this range the response would either be in the opposite direction because the inhibitory values were greater than the excitatory or in a neutral relationship where chance responses could be expected.

Noble (1961) reached the interesting conclusion that meaningfulness identified in terms of common elements helps acquisition but has no effect on transfer. One can see how associability adds many cues, e.g., projections to catch hold of, while nonassociability or meaninglessness is like trying to carry a dozen oranges without a bag. Noble's discovery of a divorce of meaning from transfer may explain why in past studies transfer (literal) has seldom generated any new alternatives in a problem situation.

Eleanor Gibson (1969) would expect positive transfer only where discrimination learned in a previous task could be employed in the new situation. Hence meaningful materials would have more discriminability and thus not only would offer no interference to learning a new task but also might have positive factors from intertask discriminability.

The point must be emphasized that as a source of new alternatives, transposition has no advantage over stimulus generalization. Within the effective range of the relationship transposing the melody to various keys leaves it fundamentally the same melody. As the Spence experiment just mentioned showed, the effective range of a ratio comparison is really quite small.

Osgood (1949) placed upon a surface the generalized results of positive, negative, and neutral transfer from various changes of stimuli and responses in a second learning. Where the responses in the second learning were identical or similar to those of the original learning, the surface tipped in the positive direction with the highest point at identical. Where the stimuli remained the same but the responses were different in the second learning, the surface tipped downward in the negative direction to express the interference scores from retroactive inhibition studies. Much of the surface was flat, meaning zero transfer from one learning to another. This integration of empirical results had not considered carefully enough the response continuum. For stimuli of different degrees of similarity Bugelski and Cadwallader (1956) found good experimental verification of the Osgood surface from their relearning scores. However, for the response continuum in all groups they detected that small changes of interpolated response interfere more with relearning than did an interpolation of an opposite response, as one would expect from the Osgood surface. The Skaggs-Robinson hypothesis fits the Bugelski and Cadwallader empirical data much better than does Osgood's theoretical surface. With the positive transfer along a continuum reduced then to the trivial case of identical responses, one can better appreciate the limitations of stimulus generalizations as a source of fresh alternatives. Any moderate change in responses on interpolated learning develops an interfering retroactive situation.

Another theory of literal association for transfer derives new alternatives through mediation. According to this view, the new alternative is approached through an intermediary. For example, if a person has learned A — B and B — C, the learning of A — C will be easier for him than for one without this prior experience. But is A — C really new? Or is it the combination of the A — B and then starting again with B, B — C? Does not the learner, confronted with known elements, attempt to retrieve chains of association starting with either one or another part, and one part leading to another? Not only simple chains as already given but also reverse chains and stimulus equivalence and response equivalence (e.g., the logical relation two things equal to the same thing are equal to each other) have been tested with some success, but four-stage paradigms have failed to produce associations different from those produced by chance (Jenkins, 1963). The reasons were ascribed to insufficient strength in the stages of the paradigm. However, the directionality factor apparently must be considered when there is no proximity. Even though Russell and Storms (1955) demonstrated that the mediation paradigm can also be applied to life experience associations, how close does that bring a new alternative needed for a problem situation? One may trace backward an uncommon association by such paradigms but for only short sequences. Also, these commonality associations are apt to be the very ones already tried, with a new alternative still to be found. The mediationists expect too much from simple mechanical surface continuities or probabilities entirely dependent on associative strength. They have failed as yet to show experimentally how the really new gets associated.

Skinner and his followers have shown how relatively easy it is to make one act the contingent discriminant s_D for the next in the series. For such a long series with even the white rat one simply needs to start with the last act and then gradually make each in the series the contingency for the subsequent act, e.g., the pressing of the food lever is made contingent on climbing a ladder to the platform where the lever is, and the ladder made available only by turning a wheel (Skinner, 1969).

After Greenspoon offered evidence that verbal reinforcement and extinction could change the emission rate of classes of free associations, Maltzman (1960) showed that the proportion of unusual or novel associations could also be manipulated by selective reinforcement. He claimed that the method indicated a trainable basis for creativity. Mednick incorporated a modification of the Maltzman method into his Remote Association Test (RAT). An experiment by Caron et al. (1963) examined the relevance as well as the uncommonness of the associations produced by the Maltzman procedure. They found it possible to get emission of six uncommon associations every ten seconds when the subject was instructed not to repeat himself. The association also showed a tendency to be relevant in a *general* way but nonetheless it had a negligible effect on problem situations which need new alternatives of *specific* relevance. Maltzman had contended that relevance and uncommonness of association are subject to the same laws.

A method fundamentally like Mednick's forcing the emission of alternatives has been given the name of "lateral thinking" by Edward De Bono (1967). He combines it with certain shock techniques, like emphasizing that you get more innovative ideas with humor than with reason and that such ideas are out of date as soon as they are perceived. While the De Bono proposals have been propagated in the business press, e.g., American Telephone and Telegraph's *Bell,* a critical experimental test like Caron's for the Maltzman method has not yet been published.

However, the results from "brainstorming" may be pertinent. This technique, first developed at Yale by Osborn, used an uncritical social situation to foster a creative atmosphere for invention and for new ideas and at first seemed very promising. Although group "brainstorming" was credited with the invention of a multipurpose home device (Osborn, 1957), the experimental testing of the method allows less sanguine expectations. Taylor et al. (1957) found that individuals working alone actually produced a significantly higher number of unique ideas than did the brainstorming group.

When seeking relevant new alternatives, social facilitation, forced emission of different alternatives, and random free associations have all been found wanting when transfer to new situations is the criterion. The Maltzman, Mednick, Osborn, and De Bono approaches all probably work *within* a memory whorl as variants of stimulus generalization and are subject to its limitations on creativity. In chapter VII the problem is approached through my perceptual theory.

Figure 7 lets one see how literal transfer can occur in three ways, the most common of which is probably stimulus generalization whose equivalence range determines the limits of getting the *same* response. In the diagram this is the case where the outer shell of a whorl is mistaken for the nodal core. Second, on the response side the range is as wide as the motor organ system and as the bisymmetry of the body allow a parallel effect. Everyone knows that while one may learn to write his name with his right hand, he can also write it with a pencil held in his left foot. Third, that response pattern which is a correct use for a particular memorial informa-

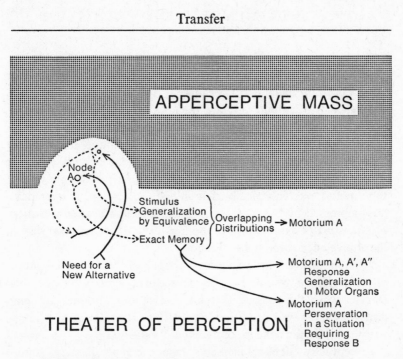

Figure 7. The incapacity of literal transfer to generate new alternatives.

tion may be perseverated in as a stereotyped solution for quite different new situations. In none of the three exemplars of literal transfer can a new alternative appear.

The equivalences of stimuli and responses in prior and later learnings have such a narrow range, shown in the generally flat Osgood surface, that new alternatives or adjustments in novel situations are improbable. The ratios of transposition show the Gestalt variety of transfer with little better promise. And in a changing world where can one find Thorndike's identical elements?

The widespread failure of transfer to answer the Hilgard and Bower (1966) question "Does learning one thing help you learn something else?" gains special significance when one checks what various learning theorists have concluded about the problem. All except Tolman and the Gestaltists are classified by Hilgard and Bower as having a position that reduces to Thorndike's identical elements or to stimulus or response generalization. Most expect little transfer. Skinner calls generalization "induction" but indicates a position much like Thorndike's. Hull differentiated between equivalences of stimuli and equivalences of response along a generalization gradient. Although Guthrie, like Thorndike, accepted that transfer was fundamentally carried by common elements, he thought the process was evoked by kinesthetic stimuli. For the Functionalists transfer was always of concrete performances and the amount was empirically determined. Pavlov in his later days was impressed by the way the language system allows substitution of one word or expression for another. Freud, too, saw transfer as the equivalence reactions to symbols.

Tolman evinced little interest in transfer, but as a cognitive psychologist he would, like the Gestaltists, expect considerable transfer when the subjects face no obstructions in observing relationships. How well cognitive formulations provide for new alternatives will be the concern of chapters VI and VII.

Perceptually, identical elements, response generalization, stimulus generalization, and mediation are all fundamentally forms of retrieval of the original response or some part of it. In stimulus generalization the relatively small increase in the number of stimuli capable of eliciting the original learned response is a matter of blunderings like malapropisms or other inadequate discriminations. Cross education would never have been taken as the laboratory model for transfer if it had been realized that the hand does not learn to trace the star pattern in mirror drawing but that such an experience with one hand modifies the usual eye-nervous system-hand perceptual relationship to such an extent that transfer to any of the learner's members including the other hand becomes probable.

The hopes for the use of transfer as a means of applying old learning in new situations have been repeatedly dashed on the rocks of critical experiments. Another approach, to be discussed in chapter VII, will deliberately work outside the literal, close to memory situation that transfer has been conceived of in traditional psychological experiments and theory.

VI PERCEPTUAL-COGNITIVE THEORIES OF TRANSFER

For now we see through a glass, darkly
I Cor. 13:12

Almost from the first the literal theories, like identical elements, met opposition from those who could accept neither their dictum of little transfer nor their avoidance of the higher mental processes when looking for transfer. Judd suggested that Thorndike and his associates ought not to have expected much transfer. "The nature of generalization is such that no simple formula like that of the presence of identical elements is remotely adequate. Generalization is a type of organized mental reaction; it depends on creative synthesis" (Judd, 1932).

Judd's experiment with ten-year-old boys throwing darts at a target under shallow water showed that there was no more rapid original learning for the experimentals who were told the principle of refraction than for the controls. However, when the depth of the water was changed, the controls took as many trials and made as many errors as they had originally, as though it were an entirely new problem. The experimental group which knew the principle rapidly adjusted to the new situation.

Unfortunately, the methodological details of Judd's experiment were not specific enough to make replication easy. Hendrickson and Schroeder (1941) found a less dramatic difference when the problem was adapted to firing an air rifle at an underwater target.

They raised the question whether the children in the experimental group really understood the principle told them and whether this failure might explain the relatively sparse transfer. Only the group that had the implications spelled out transferred at the 5 per cent level to a changed depth. On the more complicated level of college courses, Tyler (1936) reexamined students a year after the original final examinations. Tyler wanted to find out what supported the assumption that memorization of facts would produce ability to transfer and use the facts. For a wide range of courses three special examinations were developed: first, to test recall of facts taught in a course; second, to test recall of principles taught and their transfer to new situations; and third, to test ability to draw inferences from data that the students had never seen before. The correlations between scores on the tests requiring recall of information and those requiring recall and application were low, yet those between simple recall and the test of ability to make inferences from new data were even lower. The correlations between drawing inferences and the tests requiring recall of principles and transfer to new situations were also low but the range of scores fell between the other two. As he concluded, "Emphasis on recall of information does not guarantee the development of the higher mental power of drawing inferences." In surveying these tests Judd (1936) agreed that "if the higher mental processes are really to be cultivated, learning conditions appropriate for their cultivation are necessary." Results like Tyler's would seem to give definitive support to Judd's cognitive approach to transfer, but problems about kind and method of presentation persisted and only a moderately better score on inferences resulted from the teaching of principles.

First, does it make a difference whether the principle is given to the subjects or whether they have to derive it for themselves? I (Haslerud, 1968) gave subjects various amounts of specific and general guidance beyond a coded example for each of ten sentences, all of which were coded differently but all of which belonged to the same general family of codes, e.g., "substitute systematically for certain letters" as the general family but with different letters used in each example. The dependent variable was the performance a week later on the same ten codes as in the original experience and twenty others from two other families of codes as given in thirty multiple-choice encoded problems. All groups whether guided or deriving for themselves did significantly better than the controls who got only the thirty multiple-choice problems, but no difference on the whole separated the guided and deriving, although some subgroups favored one or the other. The result of this very extensive test of the problem of guidance is at about the median of studies by others. Since transfer is at times possible with either derived or given principles, I drew the conclusion that some more fundamental factor must be at work when transfer did occur. This factor is suggested in chapter VII.

Another aspect of the problem of using principles was developed by Hendrix (1950). With a mathematical principle she found that a principle discovered independently and left unverbalized was more transferable than was the problem which was verbalized after self-discovery. Premature verbalization tended to restrict the extension of the principle, even when it was stated correctly. From her avocational training of riding horses where she discovered the value of self-discovery on the part of the horse of how to do a particular pacing, she helped perfect an analogous method for the University of Illinois Mathematics Project. She also developed by demonstration and film ways to teach mathematics instructors to use the method. The Hendrix dictum about premature verbalization still implied a neo-Juddian approach because the emphasis remained on the principle.

Judd (1936) emphasized that mathematics and language involve the use of principles par excellence. He showed that these higher mental processes are systems of general ideas which can transfer because of the abstract conceptualizations one can derive from them and therefore the schools should concentrate here. He contrasted with them the meager transfer of particular experiences which obtains in the animal world. That the higher mental processes have great potentialities is supported by experimental instances in Judd's book and in more recent journals. But that this happy result is not invariably present can be shown by other studies which, for example, show geometry classes that did not transfer to better logic scores.

Much of the trouble may be in the instruction or formulation of a principle. Hilgard et al. (1953, 1954), replicating and extending the Katona card trick experiment, found great difficulty in transmitting a hint or ideas of a principle for solving the problems. They also discovered that even when subjects knew a principle, they might temporarily forget it or carelessly not perform according to it.

That a principle offers a favorable condition for later application and search for creative alternatives is well supported. However, as was mentioned earlier in this chapter, a contingent factor may account for those occasions when a principle does not suffice. Also learning a principle is not something perceptually homogeneous. It can vary all the way down from a complex scientific model to a simple relation between pairs of stimuli.

When Köhler (1925) observed chimpanzees on the island of Teneriffe learning problem solutions that supported a Gestalt point of view, he forced the psychological world to reconsider the adequacy of the mechanical Thorndikian trial-and-error paradigm for learning. Köhler at first left the impression that the experiments on transposition in hens demonstrated the same Gestalt principles as the *umweg* (roundabout) and tool-using experiments with chimpanzees. He said that transposition in the earlier period of Gestalt psychology had been taken as evidence of higher mental processes, i.e., the wide range within which a melody may be transposed to different keys and remain apparently the same melody. Later, he felt that organization was such a fundamental factor for all life that it must be due to "elementary dynamics of the nervous system" (Köhler, 1947). Hence he was not surprised to find even lower creatures like birds and rats exhibiting it.

In chapter V transposition was interpreted as stimulus generalization of ratios. To respond to "darker than" or "heavier than" or to a Weber fraction of 10/12 instead of 5/6 behaviorally is no more difficult than to respond to what seem to be equivalent or nondiscriminable stimuli on a continuum, e.g., when a male responds "red" to a wide range of wavelengths between orange and the long end of the spectrum. Spence (1942) and Brown and Overall (1958) have demonstrated that whether subjects learn absolute or relative responses depends on how the problem is broached.

Köhler's experiments with the chimpanzees, however, were not a mere extension of a ratio from earlier learning but involved a reperception of the problem situation. The results were dramatic. He found some situations in which, instead of the usual saw-toothed decline of errors or time, there was a precipitous drop in errors after some trial and error. This was followed by no regression in the performance which continued at an efficient level. Moreover, in contrast to the stupid lack of transfer which Thorndike had found in his cats, Köhler's chimpanzees often would respond swiftly and without error from one similar situation to another.

Köhler found individual differences, of course; not all chimpanzees were insightful, or any, all the time. The chimpanzee named Sultan generally succeeded while Rana was limited to trial and error or to insights too partial to be effective. Köhler observed that Sultan had a tendency after trying his normal repertoire of skills and finding none adequate to back out of the problem situation to a corner where he quietly, chin cupped in his hand, contemplated the situation from a new and wider perspective. When the goal and the means were then included in a single perception, e.g., a box and the suspended fruit, his face would light up, he would rush to the box, move it under the fruit, and mount it to get the banana. Because to Köhler this behavior looked like an Archimedes-type discovery, he called it insight.

That the reperception of the means-goal relationship was the necessary condition for exhibiting transferable insight was demonstrated by putting the means, e.g., the box, out of sight in another room or at least in such a position that it could not be seen at the same time as the goal. Even Sultan could not solve such problems. Alpert (1928) found that human children also were unable to solve such problems until they developed some language. Apparently a child using a word can bring the absent means into conjunction with the frustrating goal. For instance, the child, after futile efforts of jumping and reaching for a suspended toy, might suddenly say, "I want chair."

Because his chimpanzees came to him nearly mature, Köhler had not been able to specify another necessary condition for insight. Birch (1945) showed that young chimpanzees did not put together two shorter sticks to rake in food that was a distance greater than the length of one stick from their cage. However, after an opportunity to play with the sticks and learn something about their properties, nearly all could combine the sticks as means and exhibit the characteristics of insightful problem solving in a new situation.

Although Köhler's research on insight in both the *umweg* and tool situations indicated some generality for his concept of insight, he still left the problem largely empirical. How to recognize insight and how to increase the rate of it were left undetermined except as specifications of the problems he had used. For example, when Sultan invented how to use a several-meter stick to vault with and to climb to a high lure, the other chimpanzees imitated him. If given too short a pole, the more intelligent chimpanzees "would look up [at the suspended fruit] and then throw away the pole, or at most make one attempt and then give up. Not so Rana," called stupid by Köhler; she repeatedly tried to climb the too short jumping pole. Köhler undoubtedly did not weigh enough the previous learning and such personal characteristics as unexcitability as factors in insight. He also did not have the results of comparable experiments on human children. Sultan shifted himself to get perspective while children with some vocabulary could manipulate the elements of the problem mentally (Alpert, 1928).

Out of Tolman's University of California laboratory came another cognitive approach to the search for alternatives in problem solution. Krech (1932) found that even white rats refused to accept chance and irrationality as a basis for perception of the world. He found that when the rats were placed in a four-unit linear maze with light-dark and right-left as possible cues at each choice point, and the locking of the doors for each unit was determined by chance, they behaved in a systematic way which he called "hypothesis behavior."

Krech's rats would from time to time drop their "hypothesis" and take up another since the reinforcement was, of course, random. In the normal learning situation with a definite prescribed pattern, the organism, after it has been reinforced, leaves its position habits and other irrelevant "hypotheses" of the presolution period and settles onto the required pattern. However, an organism, which has been limited, say, by extensive brain injury, may become very fixated upon some concrete feature of the situation or its first "hypothesis."

As a paradigm for perceptual alternatives, Krech's hypothesis concept has promising features since the constant organizing and reorganizing tendencies cannot be neglected. Nevertheless, the shifts are sometimes erratic and sometimes obviously noninsightful, e.g., in extended position habits. While "hypotheses" could account for some new alternatives, the stalling on others raises questions on what promotes meaningful changes to perceive different and more significant aspects of a problem.

An examination of problem solving will reveal that there is always some hypothesis—at least a stability hypothesis that the world on the next trial will be much the same as that on the previous one. With ambiguous stimuli such as the Rorschach ink blots, or with a free maze where right and left alternative paths at a choice point are equally available, one can detect hypotheses behaviorally (Haslerud, 1953). Another instance has come from the Cognitive Center at Harvard where it was found that decision making involves the adoption of a strategy which is apt to be persisted in if successful (Bruner et al., 1956). With failure, the organism equipped with a normal repertoire will try out a new strategy.

Miller, Galanter, and Pribram (1960) helped to make acceptable again discussion of cognitive factors that had been neglected in behavioristic formulations. Their TOTE schema also introduced the idea of cybernetic feedback to psychological theorizing. They helped psychologists see that it was retrieval, not storage, that offers difficulties in learning. However, except for the use of a Plan in more than one situation, they have little to say about the problems of transfer, except as it relates to memory. The Plan was defined as "any hierarchical process that can control the order in which a sequence of operations is to be performed." Their idea of transfer seems a kind of "identical elements" of a congruent order. Although the project deals with covert Images and Plans and Metaplans, its emphasis is on "reenactment" generated according to certain rules. They actually offer little help in our quest for a way to generate *new* alternatives outside the rules for memory. Indeed, while all the earlier and later perceptual-cognitive theories of transfer have given hope for a creative kind of transfer, their formulations stop short of specifying the conditions necessary for securing that result.

VII NEW ALTERNATIVES WITH PROJECSCAN

I will go then beyond memory . . .

St. Augustine

How can one transcend his memory and get out of the rut of his practiced associations? A few creative, original individuals have succeeded in doing this from time to time. Their scarcity in any culture has made many conclude that creativity is a "given" ability and that little can be done to teach it. That rigid, unstimulating conditions may retard or even completely inhibit the tendency is generally agreed, but not much has been found to encourage the belief that there can be any positive nurturing.

Perhaps Terman's identification of high academic intelligence with genius was a blind alley. He and others should have reexamined the premise when volume II of *Genetic Studies of Genius* indicated a wide variation from IQ's of 200 down to close to 100 for 282 individuals widely regarded as historically significant geniuses. These IQ's were estimates made from the level of drawings and letters produced in early childhood. More recently, Getzels and Jackson (1962) have developed tests of hypothesis making and of production of variations. When these are correlated with conventional Binet-type tests of academic intelligence, the relationship is close to zero, i.e., random. One could interpret these results as supporting the idea that innovative capacity, while independent of intelligence, is a special ability, possibly inherited.

An alternative hypothesis might emphasize instead that an extrapolative set learned somehow by those with average or better general intelligence could account for the surveyed experimental results. The sporadic appearance of creativity might mean that although formal education either did not know how to encourage or neglected to foster this kind of activity, certain individuals discovered for themselves how to free their associative process to make full use of their Apperceptive Mass.

A favorable social climate may seem to increase creativeness by stimulating an interest in invention, by developing a general confidence that solutions can be found, and by encouraging (or even tolerating) those who turn up a new idea. Factors such as these may account for reputed Yankee ingenuity in the eighteenth and nineteenth centuries when an extraordinarily large number of new machines and ideas were produced by Eli Whitney, Nathaniel Hawthorne, and others. This environmental explanation, however, can fit either the conventional hereditary or the learning self-discovery theories. The social conditions in New England may simply have maximized the number of inventors by allowing more to develop without affecting the potential number at all.

Neither does a study of recognized geniuses provide evidence strong enough to choose between the two theories. That geniuses start their inventiveness early (Lehman, 1953) could fit a learning-perceptual model as well as a hereditary one. Similarly, Hutchinson (1949) found individuality rather than any general factors of background, education, or procedures employed characterized his group; the interviews with 250 significant artists, writers, and inventors on how they got original ideas revealed about as many differences as there were persons.

The present chapter outlines as part of a perceptual theory of after-learning that section dealing with creative transfer (creativity). If the theory is sound that the perceptual processes operate in the same way on the overt environment as on the covert internal world of memory and its variants, even creativity ought to have specifiable perceptual conditions. Then, instead of depending on an occasional individual to discover these for himself, they could be taught. More people could learn to be creative and creators could learn to be productive more of the time. Paradoxically a *general* perceptual theory of creative transfer is required to provide understanding of the *individuality* that Hutchinson perceived in his creative thinkers. Morris (1951) revealed that even retarded children can become more creative with a gestalt-like emphasis on meaning and insight in their learning.

One does not get something from nothing. Even in the simple matter of conditioning, the classical case starts with an already functioning Unconditioned Stimulus → Unconditioned Response, and an operant or instrumental conditioning with emitted responses. Creative transfer must come somehow from the Apperceptive Mass of the individual. The problem fundamentally can be reduced to the manifestation of at least one alternative to a habit or to a conventional way of thinking. Not everyone can, like the seventeenth century hero Cyrano de Bergerac in Rostand's play, invent on the spur of the moment seven ways to get to the moon. Guilford (1956) has called this divergent thinking. When Rieman and Lobachevski challenged Euclid's theorem that one and only one parallel to a line can be drawn through an external point, their novel ways of perceiving the subject opened the whole field of non-Euclidian geometry.

The new alternative may sometimes be no more than a fresh method of formulating a statement. Polya, a mathematician, showed how the solution of mathematical problems—and others too—can be aided by planning first to make clear to oneself an understanding of the problem. Basically this means expressing what is given and what unknown is sought. He suggested ways to search one's memory for similar problems, but if that fails, to reformulate the problem to see if an alternative method may be more fruitful. He demonstrated real psychological insight in such assertions as "We work hard to extract something helpful from our memory, yet, quite often, when an idea that could be helpful presents itself, we do not appreciate it, for it is so inconspicuous" (Polya, 1945). Habituation and repetition of the expected retrieval often drain an association of meaning.

Even in a static world, dull repetition and memorization cannot preserve the past. Meaning vanishes when relationships are not verified and revivified by attention and decision. Galen's discoveries about neuroanatomy, recopied and repeated during the Middle Ages, eventually came to mean even the opposite of what he had taught so that the true separation of sensory and motor nerves had to be rediscovered by Bell and Magendie.

H. Stuart Hughes in a lecture on Oswald Spengler at the University of New Hampshire on March 11, 1961, explained that history needs to be rewritten constantly to communicate with a new generation and that torn between fallible immediate description of what is important and fragmentary recall, its deeper insight may be accessible solely in analogies and poetical allusions.

Only understood knowledge and principles are contextual enough to allow recognition of related problems and new alternatives. Saugstad and Raaheim (1960) found that in a Duncker embedded type of problem when his subjects had the necessary information and understood it, there was no difficulty with its 100 per cent availability at the time of application. However, Burack and Moos (1956) revealed that existing relevant knowledge does not inevitably guarantee its use on an immediate problem. Not even examples and demonstrations helped about half of their group and three-eighths of the group had not reached the solution despite three hints graduated from the abstract to the concrete. Apparently, one needs also to enlist the creative perception of the subject so that he can "see" the relation of his information to the problem.

Figure 8 presents an interesting example of how behavior is modified by the kind of information available to the subject. With a twelve-unit unilinear maze in which the first four units are prescribed with culs-de-sac to one side and the four goal units are to the opposite side, the free (neither side made a blind alley) units provide a sensitive measure of whether the behavior there is dominated by perseveration from the entrance turns or by anticipation from those near the goal. An animal like the rat that cannot count and whose orientation to some outside constant stimulus is con-

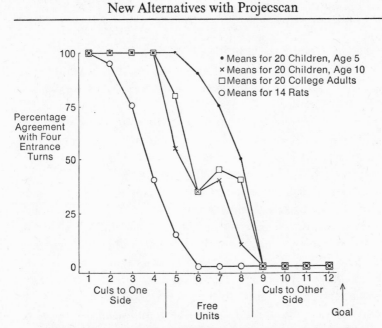

Figure 8. For rats and human subjects the interaction in the middle free units of a 12-unit unilinear maze of perseverative and anticipative information. Summarized for 3 criterion trials for human subjects from Takemoto et al. (1957) and the concluding trials 11–20 for rats from Haslerud (1945).

trolled by the covered bilaterally symmetrical maze has only the kinesthetic information from the last turn before the reinforcing goal. By Trial 10, rats were so completely affected by the goal turns that all the free units were to that side and even the third and fourth entrance units regressed from earlier correctness (Haslerud, 1945). On the contrary, young Japanese children, hand guiding a little car as they walked alongside a trenchlike maze of the same pattern, soon avoided the culs-de-sac at both entrance and goal regions but in the free units tended to perseverate the entrance turns until they got near Unit 9 for the beginning of the four goal units. Japanese college students shifted more casually from entrance to goal sides but still more perseveratively than anticipatively. When a small finger stylus maze was used in a second problem with subjects blindfolded, more trials were required to reach the criterion but the generally perseverative tendency was still present as can be seen in Figure 8, especially for the five-year-olds. Follow-up questions about cues used reveal that 70 per cent of the adults and half the ten-year-olds counted while the remainder reported "ambiguous" cues (possibly "stretch" from an orienting position). The younger children could not say what cues they used. The ten-year-olds and the adults also reported insight into the problem early in the trials (Takemoto et al., 1957).

That it is the kind of information available and not a contrast between rats and human beings which makes the difference was clarified by Spragg's experiment (1934). In a finger sixteen-unit unilinear maze with all correct turns to one side and the sixteenth to the opposite side, his blindfolded human subjects when they counted or especially oriented themselves produced curves with few anticipatory responses. However, when these factors were controlled by making the problem a temporal maze, placing it around the periphery of a bicycle wheel, and asking subjects to avoid counting, their curves approximated the goal anticipatory frequencies exhibited by his rats on a comparable problem.

In at least two places that I know of, a traveler can experience the limitation on information a rat has in a maze. On a cloudy day at Hampton Court garden in England where the hedge walls of the maze are higher than an adult, one regresses rapidly from insight. In the mazelike corridors of Chanchan, the Chimú civilization made the confusion and the anticipatory errors of invading enemies their "horizontal" defense. Even today as one walks through the many square miles of ruins near Trujillo, Peru, he can experience in the endless succession of narrow corridors and blind alleys how a man will clutch at any information—time, counting, a "stretch" from a known position—and when these prove unavailing, how he will feel very lost indeed.

To proceed from the known by small, perseverating steps seems the natural, safe way. However, perseveration can give only more of the same, and if the need is for new alternatives, these timid extrapolations will not find them. Neither is simple goal anticipation adequate. A very strong goal gradient can induce anticipations that are nonadaptive as Spragg (1934) indicated and as I

(Haslerud, 1945) showed when I pointed out that what had been learned in the entrance units can actually deteriorate from an advancing goal gradient.

Contrast with the preceding a bold projective leap into the undetermined region of the Perceptual Future. The placement of the problem in a context of freedom allows new relations to be explored. The reader must recognize that only relationships can be labile. As long as one is tied to a concrete literalness, transfer will be minimal. The projection outward also increases possible contexts. The freedom and shedding of associative inhibition from a projection into the Perceptual Future provides more than just a permissive, noncritical situation as in "brainstorming." Osborn's results increased quantity of associations but not always relevance (Osborn, 1957). What the present theory aims at are new and relevant alternatives.

The behavior of a good reader reading unfamiliar material suggests a paradigm for creative transfer. The long saccadic jumps between the restricted points of fixations along the line of print characterize the good reader; word-by-word progression, the poor reader. The good reader projects ahead a plausible meaning on the basis of the previous context and anticipates what he ought to see at the next point of fixation. Only if the anticipation does not match the previous context must he regress to try the process again. The poor reader shows an inordinate number of regressions because he has not become expert at confident and insightful extrapolation. It is obvious the good reader is engaged in a creative problem-solving activity; an extension of his procedure could give him a head start on general creativity.

A study of the history of the habits of good reading would be interesting. It probably could not be practiced, let alone be imagined, until good printing permitted effective saccadic leaps in sufficient context. One-word additions to previous context achieve a low plateau of meaning (Miller and Selfridge, 1950), but for new relevant alternatives, one needs more context and more flexibility to organize the meaning. Silent reading also had to overcome the suspicion that the capacity was due to witchcraft (statement made

August 3, 1969, by Dr. Harry Kay at the concluding addresses of the Nineteenth International Congress of Psychology). Also, the appearance of secular newspapers and books made the individual word less important than when the sacred words of the Bible were the only reading. A member of a monastic order in another country reported to me that he had been so indoctrinated to stop and meditate on each word in his religious texts that reading of modern psychological books had required learning an entirely new skill. Curiously, the new skill seems limited to English, the language in which most of his secular books are written.

What kind of theory of transfer can be developed from the good reader's paradigm? Since memory needs to be specific and faithful to its original, it provides the opposite of the conditions of free, varying perspective within a frame of relevance. Such flexibility is only possible if attention can focus on the relations among the memorial givens. The associational ruts are got out of by deliberate projection outside the memory into the Perceptual Future. From this outside perspective the learned materials can be surveyed from new foci. Therefore, while there is nothing new in the separate items, each capable of its own specific retrieval, something new may be available from the new perspective.

The Perceptual Future is a construct that includes those temporal and spatial situations not yet determined. Since the perceptual theory postulates the discreteness of each memory whorl in the Apperceptive Mass, the Perceptual Future could be in the interstices between whorls as well as in cognitive regions not populated with memory whorls.

My theory's emphasis on relationships within a new context as the basis for creative transfer brings to mind Titchener and Boring. Although Titchener is associated by many with his method of analyzing experience into psychological elements, he recognized in the process of synthesis that meaning psychologically is always the context of two or more sensations. He even went so far as to say, "Originally, meaning is kinesthesis." As for language, he maintained that "words themselves, let us remember, were first bodily attitudes, gestures, kinesthetic contexts" (Titchener, 1921). The present theory finds a low order of context in the interaction of any need and the attendant feedbacks, but a special, creative newness in the context of two or more memory whorls from the perspective of a centrifugal set in the Perceptual Future.

Boring (1933) did not use the term *information,* but his emphasis on discrimination of relations for both attention and learning anticipated much of the present theorizing in perception and cognition. He asserted, "Attention and consciousness are almost synonymous, and selection is the fundamental principle of both." My perceptual theory differs from Boring's by relating the attentional-discriminative activity to the needs of the organism manifested in the construct, the Theater of Perception, rather than to his concern for correlating brain and consciousness. Also his sparse discussion of transfer included only the literal transfer which Ebbinghaus found in the remote associates of his derived lists. The theory introduced here differentiates that literal transfer from creative transfer (projecscan).

Motivation alone will not produce new alternatives. In fact, too strong motivation may actually stereotype behavior. While the activity increased by mild motivation may result in some random variation and may have some usefulness in original learning, retrieval of memories needs less tension; projecscan searches for new alternatives will not succeed without intermittent relaxation.

Figure 9 contrasts the ordinary goal and its enclosed centripetal process with a projected goal and its centrifugal expansiveness in the Perceptual Future. Reperceiving the attained goal as incomplete helps to project the new goal ahead in a centrifugal search for the elusive copestone. The transferring strength of the goal can be measured at various distances from it by the anticipative effect on prior learned reactions or on not yet determined situations. Its curve is a convex depreciating exponential $y = k(1 - e^{-x})$. For rats in a bilaterally symmetrical unilinear maze, x is the number of the maze unit counting from the beginning (Haslerud, 1945). Probably for any situation uncomplicated by interferences, including man's anticipations as in Spragg (1934), the curve would hold. The opposite tendency, perseveration, also has an exponential curve

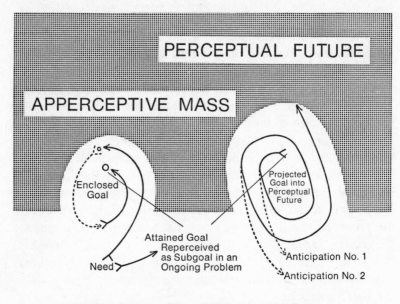

THEATER OF PERCEPTION

Figure 9. Reperceiving an attained goal as a subgoal and projecting into the Perceptual Future the problem and its further goal, with anticipations as spinoffs from the centrifugal searching.

but of the form $y = ke^{-rx}$. This concave form fits the rapid decline of perseverative influence, e.g., little persistence of entrance turns on subsequent free units for rats, and even for man if no opportunity arises for special orientation (see p. 70). This concave curve fits the transferring function of the known (attained) goal approached by centripetal approximations while the projected, still to be determined and searched for goal evokes the powerfully transferring anticipations depicted in the equation $y = k(1 - e^{-rx})$, as shown in my experiment on bidirectional gradients at subgoals (Haslerud, 1949).

The organization in Figure 5 as an economical redintegrative device should be contrasted with Figure 10's meaningful relationship derived from a new perspective on the discrete whorls. Along with the other feedbacks from the individual whorls, the new

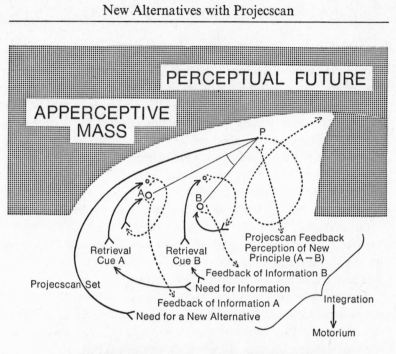

THEATER OF PERCEPTION

Figure 10. Through centrifugal projecscan set, reperception of discrete memory whorls under a unifying principle.

alternative as an outcome of the centrifugal projecscanning integrates with the original need for information before dispatch to the motorium. With practice in the centrifuging skill ever wider ranging focuses may eventually involve even whorls in the oldest parts of the Apperceptive Mass which had been learned without any prospect beyond memory. The associations from projecscan are always potentially relevant because it is the problem-goal that is projected and then becomes the center of the centrifugal spiraling.

What may not be readily apparent from Figure 10 is the need for a pause before the perspective P. An interval of relaxation gets one out of the centripetal memorial ruts and makes one open to perceive from a new scanning position on the centrifugal set. Although steady concentration on a point will end with one seeing nothing, the opposite of more acute observation often occurs after a relaxing moment. Some people like to have several projects at the same time because turning to the one acts as a relaxing interval for the other. "Sleeping on a problem" most probably works because of the new set the next morning rather than because one solved the problem in one's dreams. Earlier in this chapter the economical saccadic behavior of the good reader was suggested as a prototype of projecscan. The comparison can be pushed further by noting that nothing is seen during the saccadic leap; only when coming to rest momentarily at the various focuses on the line can information be appropriated. Köhler's most insightful chimpanzees withdrew from attempts at the goal to a point outside the problem where perspective on the means-goal relation was possible, and there they quietly contemplated the situation. In the Orient the adherents of Zen seek emptiness as an approach to *satori*.

Any transfer that attempts to be creative of new alternatives needs a projective-anticipative set to get the degrees of freedom that the undetermined future allows. Korzybski (1950) called man the time-binding animal. He wrote mostly about how the past can become as much of one's world as the present. But he did not make much of the possibilities of manipulating the future. The contextual theory postulates that the reason for emphasizing the importance of the future is the way perceptual transfer is stopped by end-goals. Attaining the goal but regarding it as a subgoal keeps the organism perceptually future-oriented and prevents mere transferring to the literal present.

Because the projective-anticipative search for new hypotheses and alternatives represents a different kind of retrieval, it ought to be designated by a special term. The old term *transfer* is really ambiguous because literally nothing is transferred from one place to another. Also, the word has come to connote some creative application to a new situation. Borsodi (1967) made a persuasive case for a separate term for each concept, especially necessary in science, to avoid ambiguity. That is obviously the trouble with the term *transfer*. It connotes a creativity and appreciation that none of the research in the field has supported. Instead, most follow the rather literal meaning of the word.

Several alternatives are open. One could reclaim *transfer* for the connotation that most people intend by the term and call *quasi transfer* what has generally gone by the term *transfer*. This was my first direction. However, only a concerted effort on the part of many could establish such a change. More feasible seems the idea of leaving *transfer* to the literal, usual, memory-like approach and of proposing a new term for the concept of seeking fresh alternatives and hypotheses.

From the theory of this essay a suitable term might be *projecscan*. New alternatives are sought by centrifugally scanning from the different perspective of a projection into the Perceptual Future. The neologism *projecscan* not only tells the reader what the activity is operationally but also suggests some of the creativity and application that may come from new alternatives.

Bartlett (1932) has used two terms to distinguish aspects of the memorial process. He has used *recognition* much as has been done in this book but makes it not only a judgmental but also an immediate apprehension. But what he calls *remembering* is much closer to our use of the word *projecscan*. He was so impressed by the changes in response given by his serial reproduction method that he thought memory was always a creative process. He stated this dramatically: "In recognising, the scheme or pattern . . . *uses* the organism; . . . in remembering the subject uses the scheme or pattern and builds up its characteristics afresh . . . In the former there is reaction by *means* of organized psychological material; in the latter there is *reaction to* organized psychological material."

Others who have proposed new terms to separate memory from the various meanings of transfer have been Guilford (1956) and De Bono (1967). Guilford called the specific memory functions *convergent thinking* which is like my centripetal set, and the creative functions *divergent thinking*. The specifications for each were to be found out by factor analysis of a wide variety of tests. De Bono divides thinking into *vertical*, which is logical and goes step by step from known premises. What he calls *lateral thinking* is characterized by random, unsystematic behavior but with sometimes creative outcomes.

Projecscan identifies the process of creative transfer and if used as a contrast to literal *transfer* (left as the traditional term), a better general understanding of the transfer problem would ensue. The terms of Bartlett, Guilford, and De Bono touch the transfer problem only tangentially and do not seem as appropriate as *projecscan* for the radically new meaning which will be defined in chapter XI.

VIII COGNIZING

❧ Asch (1969) contended that recognition has been misconceived as a type of memory or memory test instead of as a road to memory, its essential character. Recognition, he insists, must antecede associative recall; it is a nonassociative process based on similarity and is quite different from recall proper.

My perceptual theory agrees with Asch on the importance of recognition but sees it as a factor not only for memory but also for projecscan and even for immediate attention to information from the environment. The new theory differs with him on the value of similarity. The assumption that it is a post hoc judgment after a match has been responded to will be discussed in chapter XII.

The present theory uses the term *cognizing* because custom has preempted the word *recognition* and has given it its connotation as a form of memory. By cognizing is meant the perceptual response to the feedbacks of various sorts into the Theater of Perception. What happens when information returns is as important as the initiation of the circuit by the need for information. Such problems may range from looking for a water fountain when thirsty to the exploratory "What is it?" that Pavlov found in his dogs when novelty occurred.

Once initiated, how does the process come to an end and the

organism turn to other needs? The cybernetic circuits continue as long as the information returned is inadequate. In stereognosis one varies his reaction to the felt object until muscularly and kinesthetically there is the right "feel." Other feedback reactions are probably similar. A prototype of the process can be found in the Lawrence and Coles experiment (1954). The subjects instructed to identify words exposed at liminal speeds tachistoscopically selected from four alternatives given before or after the exposure. All might expect aid in this perceptual task from the alternatives given before exposure. The results, interestingly, showed the group given the recognition information after the exposure practically with the same advantage over the controls who were given no alternatives. Apparently readiness is not unidirectional. In the finite universe of four alternatives the subject turns to one after another of these until he reaches one that seems to fit. There is little comparison; the selection is immediate or if not, hardly better than chance. For the remembered alternatives the subject acts much as for the visibly presented ones after the exposure.

For another example, only those who knew the meaning of a nine-letter word were apt to perceive it at 1/25 second tachistoscopic exposure and to report it subsequently in unaided recall (Haslerud and Clark, 1957). However, with recognition aided by alternatives, the differences between those who knew and those who did not know the meaning were insignificant. The ease and accuracy of the recognition task make plausible the fact that it is a perceptual capacity fundamentally different from recall.

The present theory proposes that cognizing occurs in all perceptions but that in consciousness a differential emotional response distinguishes three types of feedback. Recognition is a kind of closure. Where the search has been routine and undelayed, the emotional accompaniment may be minimal but large enough to act as a cue. This anticipatory feeling can be observed before the responses of adaptation are complete—or even well begun—and can serve as the signal for concluding the search for information and for no longer inhibiting the response of the motorium. (Neurologically this is probably the motor areas and the final common path to various groups of muscles throughout the body but in the present theory cognizing simply means the end of the perceptual phase.)

Although the search for direct information involves commerce with the energies of the environment, all cognizing occurs solely in the Theater of Perception. The search initiating a perceptual system like seeing, for example, must discriminate the Gibsonian edges and gradients. Tinbergen (1951) determined by experimentally varied dummy figures that nestling thrushes recognized only forms similar to the parents which fed them, e.g., a ball with some protuberance like a beak would elicit gaping and thrusting if it were in motion and above the plane of the nestling's eyes. These types of information transmitted on the afferent part of the cybernetic circle produce an emotional awareness of form and order, or to use Eleanor Gibson's phrase "a reduction of uncertainty" (E. Gibson, 1969) as the process terminates.

Figure 11 brings together the three kinds of excursions for information from the Theater of Perception. From the environmental energies an afferent cognizing not only derives information but incites a mild emotional condition which, as has just been mentioned, might be termed a reduction in uncertainty. A similar feeling accompanies the feedback from kinesthesis. Into and back from the Apperceptive Mass a circuit initiated by a retrieval cue returns information accompanied by a moderate emotional condition of familiarity. A most impressive and often quite strong emotionality occurs during cognizing of a projecscan feedback. After the reperception of a new relationship between two memory whorls from the perspective P_1, the person exhibits surprise and excitement. An example might be the relation $2 \times 3 = 6$ in whorl 1 and relationship $3 + 3 = 6$ in whorl 2. From the vantage point of P_1, the individual perceives a surprising new relation between the two whorls—a principle that multiplication is a special kind of adding of like numbers.

Let us turn now to cognizing during retrieval from the Apperceptive Mass. The centripetal process may continue for a considerable time, with cognizing occurring during each feedback. As the

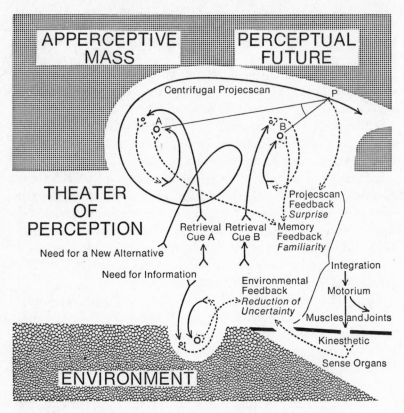

Figure 11. Cognizing continuing until search for information is terminated by reduction of uncertainty, familiarity, or surprise.

approximations continue, the question may arise how one can be sure the track of associations will lead to the desired information. Where the objective is single or overlearned, the retrieval may seem more like an instant straight line to the item rather than an approximating spiral. For example, the query "What is five times four?" results not only in an immediate "twenty" but also in a feeling of certainty, "This is it."

Slamencka (1968) using free recall of a list of twenty-five words found a curious inhibition when one group was supplied with most of the list and the other had straight recall. Although he concluded that his results proved the independence of the items in trace storage, apparently the cognizing function, according to the perceptual theory, finds familiarity only with its own retrieval plan. An imposed or gratuitous aid to recall thus handicaps the retrieval of a list. Cognizing becomes confused responding to attempts to fill in items not given.

With more elusive memories the final certainty may be approached by a rising gradient of familiarity. The outside of a memory whorl may give one no more than a feeling that he is "warm" or not too far from the term to be retrieved. One may recognize that this is like being in the neighborhood where you had found the attractive little restaurant whose name you cannot recall at the moment. Then as you walk down the street, you come to a winding street, hardly more than an alley, to the right. Your steps quicken because you now recall it was a small street. You see ahead near a streetlight the modest café sign before the steps leading down to the quaint door. A confident feeling of familiarity makes one certain before actually reading the sign and opening the door.

When a cognizing response confirms that retrieved information has met a need, further search out of the Theater of Perception stops. Almost like a *déjà vu* the organism begins to feel at home in a familiar situation and acts knowingly. It is not unlike Skinner's conception of listening as an emission of covert responses by the auditor along with or, better, slightly ahead of the speaker (Skinner, 1957). Should the speaker's words vary from the preemission, then the listener would say, "I do not understand." The speaker may adjust his emission and the auditor attempt again to anticipate his words. In terms of the present theory, a series of feedback loops taps the resources of the listener's Apperceptive Mass.

The white rat at a midpoint in learning often turns its head back and forth at a choice point, VTE behavior (vicarious trial and error) to use Tolman's descriptive term. Although not all experiments have supported the finding, Tolman and most others have found VTE's followed by rapid improvement in error scores. In a twelve-unit rectilinear free maze (without culs-de-sac), I found that VTE's were followed by a general change of side. If the animal had gone eight of the units to the right and had exhibited VTE behavior at several choice points, the next trial was apt to show predominant movement to the left. With a stabilized going-pattern, VTE's were extremely rare (Haslerud, 1934).

The behavior of both human and animal subjects changes visibly when a sought association has been retrieved. Probably all retrieval exhibits some feeling of familiarity, indicating that the search has been completed. Of course, not always is the information remembered accurate. The feeling of familiarity may have been aroused by an arithmetical product that was incorrect because of carelessness in perceiving the problem or even because of a lack of original good learning. The little restaurant you intended to find may actually be in quite a different location, but enough of the approximating cues have led you on to expect to find it exactly as you remembered it years ago so that you neglect or even reject contrary evidence. Literal transfer with its equivalences may be of this kind where a premature satisfaction stops the search before the optimal answer has been reached. Because the needs of the organism call the tune, one might expect an emotional-motivational cue to be part of the process—the lack, a signal to continue; the presence, a signal to change to another pursuit.

As Haslerud (1959) and Haber (1965) among others have found, familiarity permits perception at speeds and exposures considered subliminal under neutral conditions. This shortcutting of the retrieval process by familiarity contrasts with the case where the material is really nonsense as far as the particular individual is concerned. Then the retrieval loops may have to continue until they overlap exactly the original learning before the releasing-from-task cognizing occurs.

Using a technique of subthreshold summation so the subjects could not report anything from the view in the tachistoscope except when repetitions of the stimulus impoverished by too rapid exposure made it possible, the number of repetitions made a good dependent measure. Forty college subjects, equally divided according to sex, read aloud twice the first four lines of an unfamiliar limerick. Then each looked in the tachistoscope to see the last part of the fifth line, or "something else," and was asked to report anything seen. Each subject thus acted as his own control, having nine limericks with their own fifth line in the tachistoscope and nine that had an irrelevant limerick ending. The differences were significant at the <.001 level, with thirty-two out of the forty subjects showing differences in the expected direction. The report concluded, "The results point to a readiness for even subliminal cues when a projective anticipation has been established by relevant context" (Haslerud, 1959).

Because projecscan is the search for new alternatives, the organism can have none of the assurance that the approximations to a memory item give to the retrieval search, where the individual gradually recognizes he is reacting as formerly. Instead, an all-or-none cognizing must take place when the potential new information appears like the one-point contact of a tangent on a circle.

When Sultan in Köhler's Teneriffe experiments perceived a box and the out-of-reach hanging fruit as a means-goal organization, his face lighted up in the old 1918 film, and even before he subsequently dragged out the box to a place beneath the suspended fruit, the solution seemed to be sure. Sultan's facial change and energizing emotion seem analogous to the "Eureka!" that Archimedes is reported to have uttered excitedly as he ran naked from his bath where he had discovered the principle of specific gravity.

The surprise at finding a relevant alternative for a problem serves the same purpose of terminating an activity as does familiarity for retrieval. However, its more dramatic quality acts like italics to emphasize what has been found as new and apparently feasible. The exuberance does not guarantee a valuable idea but only the possibilities of a new road.

The three different emotional responses, from the mere reduction of uncertainty to the warmth of familiarity and finally to the excitement of surprise, may be no more than the conscious aspects of the completed cybernetic circuit. They may, however, represent prime cases such as Sperry (1969) mentions where consciousness as an emergent adds new properties to a situation.

IX TESTING THE ALTERNATIVES

Lovers and madmen have such seething brains,
Such shaping fantasies, that apprehend more than
cool reason ever comprehends.
Shakespeare

Unlike the teeming biological world of Malthus, all too few alternatives in information are available ordinarily for problem solving, but like Darwinian selection even these few must meet the requirements of a world of logic and relevance or be discarded. Yet skill and competence (White, 1959) also may determine whether any insight or transfer can become manifest. One may have a new idea, e.g., a theme for a novel or a painting, but lack the requisite skill to create it either for himself or for others. And, of course, inability to read at a sophisticated level, or to understand and perform certain mathematical or statistical processes, may make it impossible to perceive certain problems at all.

Retrievals from the memory whorls of the Apperceptive Mass sometimes need more verification than the warmth of a feeling of familiarity accompanying the cognizing of the incoming information. As might be expected, for most situations response follows retrieval without hesitation. At times this carefreeness receives a repulse; what you recalled and dialed resulted in a wrong number.

The verification reduces essentially to a discriminative match-mismatch (Bruner, Miller, and Zimmerman, 1955). The experiments, however, have dealt mostly with the simple, verbatim response to a stereotyped cue question, the ideal performance apparently being the letter-perfect recital from a tape activated by a specific signal. To be sure, a person can make errors negligible by spaced trials and overlearning.

In many cases ambiguity about the correctness of what has been retrieved leads to certain strategies for reducing the uncertainty. One may have a datum in hand and check his memory for corroborative evidence, e.g., "Is 1964 the right date for this?" More complex situations, like a need for a datum whose context is known, e.g., "Non-Euclidean geometry is most identified with whom?" may lead to a test of the retrieved name by checking its consistency with the context against one's own Apperceptive Mass or against a social retrieval source such as an encyclopedia. Similarly, uneasiness ("It doesn't look right") may require the aid of the dictionary or some other authority. Also, the rejection of retrieval information with "I'd recognize it, I'm sure, but now I can't seem to recall it right" may be instances where emotional or other interferences have blocked adequate retrieval.

One will notice that most of the retrievals outside the overlearned routine type are approximations that gradually have narrower and narrower cybernetic loops as the reconstruction of the original learning is approached. The loop for the overlearned type looks like a straight line but should be thought of as a searching probe from the cue into the Apperceptive Mass and then as a retrieved feedback to the Theater of Perception almost doubling on itself.

In contrast to the relative obviousness of tests for adequacy of retrieved information, the feedback from projecscan needs a test to match the novelty of the alternative. Any kind of proportional "identical elements" will fail to detect the appropriateness for the solution of the particular problem. Something more sensitive is required, something which perhaps is best expressed by the word *relevance*. Allusions, analogies, hypotheses, even extravagant figures of speech like those in Solomon's *Song of Songs* owe their relevance to how well they fit the context of a problem. Many examples from art and poetry come to mind. Of course, many problems allow an empirical test of the new alternative too.

A personal example illustrates the case. A large hole, six feet deep and eight feet long, had to be made in solid granite to put an oil tank safely underground, and moreover, had to be done without blasting to avoid cracking the nearby foundation of the house. A shovel, wedges and pry bar, heavy sledgehammer, and pick made practically no impression on the hard rock. When I came to the end of the available tools, I recollected how Hannibal had cut a path in the high Alps for his elephants by pouring hot wine on the cold rocks. On a summer day a literal translation of the method was obviously out of the question. But if rock had been cracked by a sudden change in temperature, why not heat the rock and then chill it! The new alternative struck me as so relevant to my problem that I felt sure it would work even before I built a fire and then doused the rock with cold water. The granite splintered well, and it took only a few repetitions of the process to complete the excavation.

Once an alternative has been perceived by projecscan, its future depends on being secured by a retrieval cue. A man might write himself a memo or enact some other way he favors to establish his set to retrieve. The new idea will then be available for repeated examination. The new alternative becomes a part of the Apperceptive Mass from which it was derived but in which it never existed until reperceived by the projecscan perspective.

Recall that the Apperceptive Mass consists primarily of memory whorls developed by retrieval sets and of a smaller proportion of "instinctive," "reflex," innate readinesses which derive from heredity. The new additions from projecscan will probably always be a small but especially important area of the Apperceptive Mass. With the hypothesis that the new alternative comes from a different perspective or reperception of a node in the environment and one or more memory whorls, the most adequate location for focusing the retrieval set of the new alternative is at or near its inception. This not only organizes more of the Apperceptive Mass but, unlike ordinary organization strictly connected only in the Theater of Perception, creates a potentially more volatile kind of information. One might predict that creativity would flourish on creativity.

The projecscan set selects from positions on its centrifugal spiral those perspectives that seem to provide relevant information for new alternatives: When such alternatives are later examined dispassionately, the relationship glimpsed earlier may not be evident. Who has not made a notation and afterward wondered why he had made it?

In the cold light of day the new information may need to be tried in various categorizations in order to be comprehensible. This fitting into the framework of previous knowledge indicates whether it is merely a redundant formulation of something else or really a discovery that fills a spot which needed just such an item. The internal consistency among the older and new information has to be examined because a reliably existent inconsistency would tell us that a new category had been found. Since Becquerel could not explain the exposed photographic plate by anything he knew, he postulated that some new form of radiation must come from the pitchblende.

A test of applicability may show that the new alternative does not relate to the problem at hand, though it may be a suitable idea for something else. Serendipity accounts for the happy biproducts of research where good leads are found for a new study. A coal-tar dye, for example, may have medical properties. The relevance test, moreover, may encourage one, even with an imperfect fit to the problem, to keep projecting the problem into the same general region for more adequate information.

Nevertheless, the test may be such an adequate, satisfactory solution that one can only respond with some emotional overflow, or the ideomotor response may occur almost automatically before a thorough examination of the idea has been completed. A more complex situation may have to become part of a suborganization in the Apperceptive Mass as preparation for a final adaptive response. In the present study transfer had to become part of a new way of looking at all after-learning before the distinctive features of literal transfer and projecscan could be worked out.

The projected problem may generate a new alternative that allows a hypothesis to occupy the stage of the Theater of Perception. The same kinds of tests as those for individual alternatives are made. Similarly, the death rate among hypotheses is high. A logical examination may pile up evidence against the hopeful suggestion. One should not estimate the frequency of creative projecscan by the number of final "good" ideas. One needs many alternatives to have some survive the tests of logic and relevance. Even before Freud's fundamental discovery of secondary elaboration as a factor in the transformation of the latent dream into the manifest dream, many people must have noticed the harmonizing forces within the context itself from the fragmentary notes through the first draft to the published form. A complete journal of the false starts and blunders made in forming a hypothesis, a workable procedure, the interpretation of results, and the final article in a scientific journal would reveal a precarious, far from straight-line progression to the goal.

Not every insight, even if actualizable, is necessarily an improvement on an older available response. The conventional solution may be unsatisfactory in many ways, but the apparently promising alternative may cost many times as much. Although DDT changed the history of the tropics by almost wiping out the malarial mosquito, the biological damage to fish and bird life made it a questionable method even if the mutant varieties of mosquitoes resistant to the chemical had not made the victory a short-lived one.

In order to actualize a new idea discovered through projecscan, the foundation of the skill to accomplish this cannot be overemphasized. Some of Köhler's chimpanzees had apparently reperceived that a certain problem required a structure of several boxes to reach the high lure. They would at times mount the boxes already piled and hold the final box in their hands. Even where the boxes were piled high enough, the chimpanzees, lacking engineering skill, would place each box without regard to a solid foundation or the center of gravity, and success was mostly a matter of rapidly climbing to the top to clutch the fruit before the whole edifice tumbled.

The cognitive psychologists like Tolman and the S-S Behaviorists like Guthrie who postulated that learning occurred in a single trial agreed that only with an actualizing performance could one see what had been learned. Only when the set and motivation were made favorable, even after an interval of time, could the learning be exhibited again. That too much motivation could interfere with learning and retrieval was shown in Harlow's monkeys which solved the locking device of a problem box better when it was not baited with a raisin (Harlow, 1959).

The maintenance of the requisite motivational tension may be part of the skill in actualizing. If one's skills are too largely verbal, the problem may be "solved" by simply talking about it, leaving incomplete the needed road or invention which had started the search for new alternatives. Hutchinson (1949) from his study of inventors, writers, and scientists and their methods emphasized the value of persisting in an inquiry instead of stopping with only a partial insight. The writers with some self-discipline actualized more of their ideas than did those who depended on inspiration from their new idea.

Pitting the number and relevance of alternatives provided by transfer from identical elements or from stimulus or response generalization against alternatives from projecscan for adequacy in meeting needs for the solution of new problems should provide a crucial test. Literal transfer might be expected to resemble the memory retrievals that had already been found wanting. Judges who did not know the source of the various alternatives would be asked to discriminate between the solutions that seemed relevant to the problem and those that did not. The actual solution of the problem would, of course, be the ultimate test of an alternative.

X GENESIS OF MEMORY AND PROJECSCAN

The beginning, as the proverb says,
is half the whole.
Aristotle

Since projecscan depends on a well-stored Apperceptive Mass, as was outlined in chapter VII, one first must account for the development of memory. Most behavior, as was indicated in chapter III, requires no storage. The reverberations of sensory processes for several seconds in positive and negative afterimages for vision and probably similar perseverations in other sense modalities give enough maintenance of the information during immediate apprehension in the Theater of Perception to allow the production of immediate memory. This misnomer, and its synonym short-term memory, have given rise to the postulation of a continuity from immediate to longtime memory. The perceptual theory of afterlearning, however, emphasizes the discreteness of the two concepts. The "recall" in immediate memory is just a necessary indication of the inclusions within the span of attention and might be given more reliability by some other technique, e.g., a method of recognition or selection.

Longtime memory, based in the Apperceptive Mass, is a reconstructing process (Neisser, 1967) and not a perseverative one like immediate memory. Any resemblances between the two are fortuitous; longtime memory cannot be built on a short-term model.

As part of his physiological readiness the newborn human child includes responses which can be released by certain perceptual processes, e.g., the smile at two months to stimulus of a face. Birds and animals, well supplied with such "instinctive" S-R relationships, have been studied experimentally by Tinbergen (1951). The innate retrieval cues for information on how to behave—lifting heads and opening mouths when a parent bird lights on the edge of the nest—are just as physical (slight vibration) as other information that can be perceived in the organized edges and gradients of the environment. The innate readiness also exhibits waxing and waning according to maturation and learning. Lorenz studied the tendency to follow in goslings and found that it was affected by the rapid learning and fixating imprinting process during the critical period of about fifteen hours after hatching. When only he was present during that period, the goslings would follow him and not their own species (Tinbergen, 1951). The emotional condition of disquiet or loneliness seeks out information, and the readiness in the Apperceptive Mass quickly approximates through only a few cybernetic loops the specific discrimination for the particular response. Many of the conditions for imprinting are quite specific, e.g., the visual stimulus to be imprinted is optimally at a 20° angle above the horizontal plane of a chick's eye (Smith, 1960, and personal communication).

The young child's first reactivations are the vivid, photographic eidetic images. He discovers that even when he closes his eyes, he can continue to see things and people. Freud (1957) recounted how a small child developed a tolerance for the absence of his mother by pretending in a game to hide her by occluding her from sight and then finding her again. He suggested that the image finally could comfort when the mother had gone away.

As the child grows, he has less time to "overlearn" the whole given perception of an event in the environment. He develops skill in redintegrating by parts and signals as he becomes an adolescent and adult. Piaget found in this symbolic activity a harbinger of adolescence (Berlyne, 1957).

The conditioning of signs begins slowly somewhere around one year of age. The word *mama* brings the attention of the mother and *milk* the desired drink. Such conditioning has usually provided the child with only a dozen or two such signs by eighteen months. The true language period begins with its explosive expansion of vocabulary when the child goes in search of language instead of waiting for someone to condition him. He asks, "Wa dat?" and wants to know the name of everything. Language then rapidly becomes a tool for controlling the outer and inner environment.

The use of the conditioned sign and then words in general to retrieve images and, later, information develops the cybernetic loop. The useful information becomes conditioned to the needs and then to the intent contingent to the search. Probably the centripetal set originates from a zeroing in, as outer associatives and images become contingent for those closer to the reinforcement of finding the once-learned bit of information.

During the centripetal process of establishing the intent to retrieve, tensions are probably higher than when the nodal vortex has been reached. This tendency is accentuated in children because they take a task more seriously than do adults (Koffka, 1935). Koffka reviewed a study by Ovsiankina that showed children to have a stronger Zeigarnik tendency than adults to resume unfinished tasks. However interested they had been in a particular project while working on it, the children never asked to repeat it once it had been finished. Nevertheless, for days afterward they would ask to resume an unfinished task.

At first the storage period between establishing the "intent-to-retrieve" set and the actual retrieval reinitiated by a contingent cue for the "intent" set might be short, yet the retrieval process once founded could be involved whenever needed and time would no longer be an important matter. Skinner discovered that pigeons still showed normal extinction curves after an interval up to six years when totally without the presence of an invoking discriminant.

When ordinary retrieval has been developed so that "storage" in the Apperceptive Mass is a commonplace and has passed a critical amount, the learning of projecscan can begin. A possible hypothesis traces projecscan back to saccadic eye movements and these back to a differentiation of the rapid return movement in nystagmus (J. J. Gibson, 1966). As contrasted with the slow drifting pursuit movement, the quick movement allows attention to fasten on specific points. This capacity to focus on particulars transfers easily and with hardly any awareness from exploration of the external visual field to similar jumping between immediate memory images when the eyes are closed. When the person is in revery or dreaming, the memory whorls or clusters in the Apperceptive Mass are similarly scanned. Witness the REM (rapid eye movement) behavior during dreaming (Dement, 1965). This explains why *projecscan* seems a suitable term for behavior characterized by searching for new alternatives.

With ability to project problems into the Perceptual Future on a centrifugal course to get new perspectives on clusters of memory whorls in the Apperceptive Mass, another kind of projection becomes possible, that of motivation toward a goal. An attained goal from the perspective of a future goal can be reperceived as a subgoal. This change prevents the "finality of the goal" phenomenon, a closure of the problem and solution that stops both access through retrieval cues and any kind of transfer or projecscan.

Insight, it should be made clear, can occur in immediate apprehension if the organism, e.g., one of Köhler's apes, changes its position so that the stick-means and the suspended-fruit goal can be perceived as a totality. The chimpanzee meets insuperable difficulty in adapting such perceptual shifting to his Apperceptive Mass. The human child, however, can do this when he has developed sufficient verbal retrieval cues. Alpert (1928) found in the kindergarten children tested on the Köhler problems a high correlation between increasing language and the increased quantity and level of difficulty of insightful problem solutions. Small children, nonetheless, are not really creative; they lack enough Apperceptive Mass to provide the quantum necessary for projecscan, and in addition they lack conscious control of perceptual activity. What seems very original comes from inadequate discrimination, e.g., calling a pinecone a butterfly.

We must next consider how the organism learns to respond not only to the concrete case, but to principle. Gestalt transposition is fundamentally transfer from ratio learning. The chimpanzee or child learns that the essential cue is "longer than" and becomes alert for such discrimination. From simultaneous comparisons there is a progression to successive comparisons. Eventually these become practically as easy as the simultaneous when the time interval is not too great or when the child can use a verbal mediation. After a critical amount of conditioning training to ratios, the organism can respond relationally rather than only absolutely. The Gestaltists probably made a mistake in postulating that the relational response on a wide spectrum was primary. Stimulus generalization should not be confused with ratios. Spence (1942) showed how what looks like a relational response can be explained more simply on an absolute basis, but he recognized that the child who has language can go beyond the algebraic additions of excitatory and inhibitory conditioning. He was, however, unwilling to admit the relational discrimination in animals. It was the work of Krech, Harlow, and Tolman which indicated that even animals respond to principles and hypotheses. Tolman (1932) claimed VTE to be one of the supports of a cognitive and purposive kind of behaviorism; another was "hypothesis behavior," developed most extensively by his student Krech. Harlow did the experiments which clearly differentiated simple conditioning from what he called learning sets (really hypotheses). By a genetic approach, Harlow (1959) showed that soon after birth baby monkeys are capable of learning a two-choice discrimination and can discriminate almost as rapidly as naive adults. The babies, however, are incapable of the kind of learning set response which adults can manifest after proper training. Only when the monkeys are more than five months old are their nervous systems ready to allow learning sets.

After that critical period the monkey gradually learns to respond with only six trials on any one point by using his response on the previous trial as a cue, i.e., as a contingency, for the next trial on the pair to be discriminated. Gradually the second trial on a new discrimination rises to 95 per cent or better correctness. It is as though the principle had been adopted "If not that, then this." The flexibility of the learning set includes reversal behavior too.

Although at first the most active region for projecscan is near those places where fanlike retrieval clusters have been developed, a still more active region comes into being from the fixing of projecscan by a retrieval cue. This would help explain how the creative individual becomes ever more fertile in hypotheses and new alternatives, possibly in a positively accelerated curve. One might suppose some special "aliveness" about this information as contrasted with the drab, constricted quality of simple memory. The greater sensitivity (low threshold) to new relationships underlying the growing sophistication of Sultan in Köhler's Teneriffe group of chimpanzees or of Moos at the Yerkes Laboratory in Florida exemplifies the cumulative nature of creative transfer. I have also observed a number of boys who came to the university from mountain coves where educational opportunity was limited. In the university where they somehow had "learned how to learn," an impressively accelerated increase in Apperceptive Mass and ability to use it accompanied their metamorphosis into lawyers, scientists, and teachers.

In this chapter a number of hypotheses propose how memory retrieval and projecscan originate ontogenetically and possibly phylogenetically. Since projecscan can operate only on a sufficiently large Apperceptive Mass, retrieval becomes the basic problem.

The Apperceptive Mass at birth already functions with certain instinctive readinesses, some of which, e.g., imprinting, have possibilities for the modification of the natural contingency stimulus. A sensitivity for both exact and approximate cues accompanies the innate readiness. The problem for recall of learned information resolves into how to develop an adequate cue or set for the reconstruction, since the return part of the cybernetic loop from the Apperceptive Mass is probably similar for phylogenetic and learned memories.

From projecscan as a modified saccadic visual movement the organism learns to scan the combinations of memory whorls in the

Apperceptive Mass in a manner similar to the way saccadic movements focus here and there in the external world. The direction of scanning moves centrifugally. An occasional perspective from its orbit may allow a reperception of the relation of two or more memory whorls. But that kind of skill can extend further. Once such projection has been developed, the manipulation of goals also becomes possible; an attained goal can be reperceived as a subgoal and a new goal projected into the Perceptual Future.

XI ASSUMPTIONS, HYPOTHESES, DEFINITIONS

A satisfactory scientific theory should begin with a set of explicitly stated postulates accompanied by specific or "operational" definitions of the critical terms employed.

Clark L. Hull

Each of the preceding chapters has developed an aspect of a new perceptual theory of after-learning. Short-term memory, more permanent memory, transfer, and creative transfer (projecscan) have been integrated by differentiating them from a common source in the organism's need for information to solve its problems. This chapter presents the formal structure of the theory as developed to date. The next two chapters and the epilogue examine the theoretical and practical implications and deductions of the theory.

At least five lines of evidence were either unknown or unused as a basis for the theories of pioneer students of transfer like Thorndike:

(1) The effect of motivation and emotion on the establishment and maintenance of learning and memory was little emphasized until Tolman.

(2) The gating in the reticular formation as part of the selectivity of sensory information entering the organism made untenable the puppet model with respect to the stimulus.

(3) The evidence provided by J. J. Gibson that the information from invariants in the environment was directly responsible for the constancies in perception.

(4) The cybernetic, servomechanistic model which Norbert

99

Wiener extended from mathematics to the nervous system was seized on and exploited by psychologists because of their earlier acquaintance with kinesthesis.

(5) Neisser and others changed memory from a static, depository type of function to a dynamic, reconstructing behavior.

All of these five changes in perceptual-cognitive theory have been incorporated into my perceptual theory of after-learning and have made possible a fresh attack on the problem of differentiating the conditions for creative as well as literal transfer.

The perceptual theory of after-learning can be located conceptually by relating it to the recent theorizing of others. It includes the external environment as a source of stimulus information but does not remain solely peripheral like the theory of the Gibsons (1966, 1969). Rather, it starts with the need for information and follows the cybernetic cycle by way of the attentional surges into and back from the Apperceptive Mass. The cycle is postulated to be reverberating until the information produced frees the organism from uncertainty. Neither does this perceptual theory adopt Neisser's two stages of preperception and synthesis, although it agrees with him that perception and cognition, which psychology has arbitrarily and traditionally separated, should be integrated (Neisser, 1967). Again, the perceptual theory of after-learning finds no need for Neisser's "executive" but adopts gratefully his reconstruction theory of retrieval from past traces, even though he did not carry his concept far enough to account for new alternatives—the ultimate concern of the present theory. Similarly, Miller, Galanter, and Pribram (1960) neglected creative transfer and even literal transfer, writing that they do not know where to find new ideas and alternatives except heuristically. Although their TOTE (test-operate-test-exit) paradigm, Images, and Plans can be fitted congenially into the new perceptual theory of after-learning, and although this author acknowledges indebtedness to them for liberating his thinking about perception and learning, their proposals do not go far enough.

Few psychological writers have been more consistent than Bruner in advocating that principles and organization are essential, that hypothesis making ought to be encouraged in the learner, and that learning must be such that performance goes beyond the given. With most ingenious experiments he finds certain arrangements that work, but one searches in vain for any comprehensive theory. In my review (Haslerud, 1961) of his *Process of Education* I contrasted his emphasis on discovery and the attainment of cognitive structure with the rather static conception of transfer indicated in such passages as "Transfer of principles is dependent upon mastery of the structure of the subject matter" (Bruner, 1960). He overlooks the difficulty in recognizing the relevance of a principle to the problem at hand. Along the same line Bruner ended a penetrating essay on creativity of new ideas with what seems from the point of view of the perceptual theory as insufficient advice to the advertising men he was addressing: "The problem for the creative 'ad' man (or any other creative person) is to find the combination of old ideas that will lead to new combinations" (Bruner, 1957).

When the organism is considered a *tabula rasa* and all the effective agents external, one has the attractively simple universe of the physical scientist. Unfortunately, when applied to the living and learning organism, the model fits badly. The necessity for a change in the model should have been apparent when repetition turned out to be only a secondary principle of learning (Thorndike, 1932) and when extinction trials were found to have only a small relation to the number for original conditioning (Humphreys, 1939). Taking the objective stimulus as the element to deal with, as Thorndike (1913) did with "identical elements," or its neural excitation, as Guthrie and Hull (Hilgard and Bower, 1966) did, kept creative and applicative use of learning from being more than minimal. With a shift to a perceptual model based on the *relations* between stimuli and between stimuli and the organism, many of the problems of learning and after-learning can be resolved more easily than with the alternative literal model.

Koch (1959) rightly called for those who propose theories in psychology to make explicit their assumptions and terms and to state a theory in such a manner that crucial tests can be made of it.

Since the constructs of the present theory are operationally defined, excess meaning (MacCorquodale and Meehl, 1948) has been largely reduced, and the constructs may qualify as E/C (experimentally controlled) in the Marx (1963) sense. Because the theory is a medium-level one, it integrates a large number of phenomena but makes no attempt to provide other than a psychological context. (It is not a physiological connective theory.)

Allport and Norman have systems that superficially resemble aspects of the perceptual theory of after-learning. F. G. Allport (1955) integrated previous perceptual theories by trying to provide a basis for both structural and quantitative laws. He also included many references to learning but even more to neurophysiology. To counter the conventional linear chain from sense organ to nervous system he advanced a fundamental assumption of a universal kinematic circularity. "Let us think of the series [of ongoings and events] as always coming back on itself and completing a cycle," with event-structures at the intersections of cycles. His proliferation of cycles reminds one of the prophet Ezekial's wheels within wheels.

My theory, too, is based on feedbacks but places them in the context of behavior by starting with the needs manifested in the Theater of Perception and thus avoids the ambiguities and complications of Allport's "c," "r," and "n" lays and cycles. Moreover, it does not require a gratuitous assumption of a universal tendency for circularity of ongoings. The loops occur when projective searches for information invade the environment and the Apperceptive Mass, and the returns are seen as anticipations to the Theater of Perception. The theory is also more comprehensive than Allport's because he neglected the problem of transfer.

Norman (1968) presented a theory that includes only the areas of memory and attention, but his assumptions, modeled on computer programming, point up the organismic basis of my theory. He assumes an automatic matching by sensory features of the stimulating signal and its stored representation, modulated by a "pertinence" input from a cognitive biasing factor. His system fits better the concreteness of tape or Holerith card than the searching set of a living organism with its centripetal approximations upon a bit of retrieval information or a more exact definition of an external stimulating situation. The present theory needs no assumption of automatic matching for selective attention; the immediate needs of the organism concentrate attention on the sources of information with low thresholds and continue the search until cognizing of a satisfactory resolution of the problem permits a change. If Norman were to extend his system to include the transfer problem, his essentially linear plan, despite its feedback from storage and decision point, would preclude it. That system could not produce a new alternative.

The Theory

The perceptual processes operate from the Theater of Perception in the same manner upon both the external world of stimulus energies and the internal world of memory and its variants. This general supraordinate theory rests upon a number of assumptions and can be approached and tested only through a series of subhypotheses.

ASSUMPTIONS

1. Only changing energies can be stimuli.
2. Only for the attentive and physiologically ready organism can potential stimuli become actual stimuli.
3. Only relations between stimuli can be information.
4. Informative relations can be found in both the environment and the Apperceptive Mass.
5. Learning changes discriminability and availability (as in categorization) of information.
6. The nodal trace of the cybernetic loops into the Apperceptive Mass can act like a holograph to reconstruct a whole (memory).
7. Attending can occur at only one location at a time and with limited span.

8. With delays, the level of consciousness accompanying the feedbacks into the organism rises. Innate and conditioned reflexes seldom exhibit any conscious behavior.

9. All perceptual activity occurs in the present time of immediate apprehension on the way to the firing of the motorium.

SUBHYPOTHESES

A. In the Theater of Perception the needs of the organism initiate searches for information by cybernetic loops whose feedbacks interact with the needs, the whole process continuing until needs are met.

B. The interacting process of need and of cognizing feedback which stops the searching process for information is attended by a distinguishable emotional condition.

C. The search for information goes through the sequence from environment to Apperceptive Mass to Perceptual Future as the earlier provide insufficient information and as such devices as coding, retrieval, and projection-anticipation are mastered to enter the later stages.

D. A conscious intent-to-retrieve can save as a retrieval set enough of an informative relation to allow later reconstruction of the specific memory if interferences from other information do not occur at or soon after the establishment of the retrieval set.

E. Each discrete memory nodal trace is the convergent point of a centripetal series of cybernetic loops from the Theater of Perception to the Apperceptive Mass and back again, an arrangement which makes possible literal transfer from the outer loops during the approximating retrieval.

F. The discrete memory whorls of the Apperceptive Mass can be related and organized only through overlaps of ends of the cybernetic loops in the Theater of Perception.

G. The search for new alternatives becomes possible when sufficient development of Apperceptive Mass has occurred and when sufficient conscious control allows escape from the ruts of literal retrieval by centrifugal projection of the search for information into the Perceptual Future. Through fresh perspectives from there of the Apperceptive Mass, of the environment, or of the combination of both, new alternatives are generated and fed back into the Theater of Perception.

H. The consciously controlled projection of problems and goals into the Perceptual Future and the perception of attained goals as subgoals allow control of the very needs which power the initiating perceptual processes.

I. The Apperceptive Mass eventually includes three regions which yield information in an ascending order from a region of innate readiness and conditioned responses, to a region of memory whorls saved by retrieval sets, and, most pregnant of all, to a region where new alternatives from projecscan processes have been captured into retrievable memory whorls.

J. An overt, practical solution to a nonroutine problem of an organism requires not only perception of a new alternative but also an adequate level of motivation, skills, and opportunity.

K. With development of skill in projecscan's centrifugal scanning and correlative skill in "capturing" the new information into retrievable memory whorls, it becomes feasible to use projecscan in original learning in order to achieve a growing edge in learning, better control of motivation, more useful memory, and a readier creative transfer.

L. Although feedback from both the environment and the Apperceptive Mass is attended by some awareness, it is the ultra-stimulating feedback from projecscan that leads to the emergence of an "ego," a condition favoring increased integration and control of all learning and after-learning.

DEFINITIONS

When learning, memory, transfer, and creative processes are perceived in a different light, it inevitably becomes necessary to redefine some old terms, like transfer, and to introduce new ones. Many psychological terms have had their definitions based on a literal, nonperceptual frame of reference. Thus Thorndike conceived of learning as actual bonds between neurons, and memory as the redintegration when one of the bonds was activated. His definitions assumed a neurology of discrete neurons, discrete synapses, and no feedback.

Some representative terms follow which have been redefined to stress their perceptual meanings in the context of the new theory. For several conceptions not previously identified in current psychological writing neologisms were developed, e.g., projecscan, to give each its specific designation.

After-Learning. The variety of behaviors subsequent to reaching a given criterion of learning, e.g., memory, transfer, projecscan.

Apperceptive Mass. A construct of three regions of unconscious readiness, consisting of innate propensities and the conditioning based on them; learned intents to specific recall of information from the environment and established by retrieval sets; and similar intents-to-recall but based on the creative alternatives of projecscan.

Attention. A momentary concentration of need for information in the Theater of Perception accompanied by reduction of the threshold for a narrow span of stimuli which are sought for, and by orientation of sense organs toward the stimulating figure in the environmental ground or by a parallel orienting toward a node in the Apperceptive Mass.

Availability for Perception. From the external environment, a low enough threshold. From the Apperceptive Mass, a retrieval cue which is a necessary condition for lowering the threshold into the unconsciousness of particular whorls in the Apperceptive Mass. From a projecscan focus in the Perceptual Future, a new context or perspective of two or more memory whorls in the Apperceptive Mass, or of configurations in the external environment, or of a combination of memory whorls and environmental configurations.

Behavioral Information. Those relations between size, location, or other discriminable characteristics of the environmental energies or of the Apperceptive Mass which are necessary to the organism to solve its problems.

Behavioral Supports. An operational term for those organizational and motivational aspects of after-learning, without which the behavior cannot be maintained within desired limits of variability.

Categorization. The names, orders, or other collecting devices to detect information in a large number of discrete items by which the stimulation may be brought within the subject's span of attention.

Cognition. That aspect of the perceptual-cognitive processes, e.g., thinking, dreaming, consciousness, which emphasizes the intensity and/or level of activity in the Theater of Perception.

Cognizing. The confirming emotional awareness from feedback into and interaction with needs in the Theater of Perception. From the environment this is expressed as relief from uncertainty. From the retrieval feedback the approach to or attainment of the needed specific association is attended by a feeling of familiarity. From the projecscan feedback the finding of a new alternative provokes surprise and initiates subsequent efforts to orient the new response to some familiar categorization.

Consciousness. A condition depending on the relation of feedback of information into the Theater of Perception to the meeting of needs of the organism, rising in intensity for delays and inadequate information and characterized by accentuation of attention and when beyond a critical value by the emergence of self-awareness.

Context. The organization of perceptions within which one can interpolate relationships and meanings.

Creativity. The production of socially valued new alternatives.

Feedback (Cybernetic) Loops. Initiated by the needs of the organism as manifested in the Theater of Perception and return to it with information after excursions into the external environment or the Apperceptive Mass.

Goals and Subgoals. The goal ends a behavioral episode by meeting the need which initiated and continued it. On the way to the goal small incentives may reinforce their antecedent region so well that they can be denominated subgoals. Control of the motivational process by perception of an attained goal as a subgoal and with projection ahead of a new goal represents the ultimate in projecscan.

Immediate Memory (Immediate Apprehension). The feedback from the stimulating energies of the environment, limited in extent to the span of attention and temporally to the extinction of the afterimages. This immediate apprehension represents the largest kind of activity in the Theater of Perception.

Information. Form and relationships of energies in the external environment and of the retrievable memory reconstructions from past processed information that are perceived as needed by the organism for the problem at hand. Objective, logical relationships may fail to be information for an unready organism.

Memory. A type of behavior initiated by retrieval cues which can reconstruct information similar to former but now absent learning from discrete centripetal memory whorls in the Apperceptive Mass. The prototype of this behavior is the relearning to criterion (savings method) of Ebbinghaus.

Memory Whorl. The discrete constellation of an item and its centripetal stimulus generalizations in the Apperceptive Mass. As the reapproximating retrieval process zeros in to the desired information, it goes from the clangs and superficial resemblances on the periphery to synonyms and antonyms closer in.

Motorium. The final common efferent regions and pathways in the nervous system conducting to the effector organs.

Needs. Physiological and/or cognitive states which operate through the Theater of Perception to search for information to meet the problems giving rise to the needs.

Node. Residual process or trace in the Apperceptive Mass from which, like the hologram (Pribram, 1967), can be reconstructed information similar to that originally learned.

Organization of Learning. By overlap in the Theater of Perception of a feedback loop from each of two or more memory whorls in the Apperceptive Mass, a single retrieval cue may become capable of redintegrating the information from the total number of connected whorls, and occasionally a logical and useful generalization may be perceived, but insightful principles are more apt to be obtained by the projecscan process.

Perception. Those perceptual-cognitive processes for detecting and discriminating information. The term covers more than the conventional sensory-perceptual emphasis on the sense organs and their stimulation from the environment because it also includes retrieval operations on the Apperceptive Mass.

Perceptual Future. A construct of the relationships among the memory whorls, in the interstices of the Apperceptive Mass and outside the rut-like, centripetal path of a retrieval set in a single memory whorl, and accessible only by projecscan.

Projecscan. A conscious, centrifugal, scanning set which projects a problem, hypothesis, or context into the Perceptual Future to seek new alternatives in information from the consequent perspectives which allow reperception of relations between two or more memory whorls or between memory whorls and some organization in the environment. A projecscan feedback which evokes an emotion of surprise is cognized in the Theater of Perception as both new and relevant. Whether the new alternatives are of good quality and whether they evolve into overt adjustive behavior depends on a requisite level of motivation and skill.

Relevance. The characteristic emotional response to a projecscan insight. An applicable though often nonliteral contextual relationship, e.g., figures of speech, between a new alternative solution and the initiating problem.

Stimulus. A change in quantity and/or configuration of environmental energy capable of discharging a ready sense organ. Although all information from the environment is a stimulus, the reverse is untrue.

Theater of Perception. A construct making immediate apprehension a region where all interactions occur among initiating needs, the searching loops for information into and back from the external environment and the Apperceptive Mass, and the efferent resultant toward the motorium.

Transfer. A type of behavior in which retrieval cues reconstruct information from memory whorls in the Apperceptive Mass equivalent to original learning but differing along a continuum of stimulus and response generalization. Transfer is literal and continuous like memory and unlike the creative discontinuities of projecscan.

If I were to have a definition for *learning*, it would, from my perceptual theory, have to include the following ways the perceptual processes become modified:

1. The organism enlarges its innate capacity for discrimination in the environment by categorization.

2. The organism learns how to save processed information by reperceiving it in the context of a retrieval set.

3. The organism learns how to generate new information by perceiving from a frame of reference projected beyond immediate apprehension.

4. The organism learns how to manipulate perception to affect the very needs which initiate behavior by reperceiving internal and external stimuli, by reperceiving attained goals as subgoals, and by reperceiving increasingly *sub specie eternetatis.*

5. The organism learns how to perceive in a way to develop an emergent conscious control of its own behavior and functional world as contrasted with control by chance pressures of environmental forces and organismic desires.

Barriers to Information

All information is sought from, received into, and processed in the Theater of Perception. Certain barriers obstruct the free access of information unless techniques are developed to circumvent these obstacles. Table 2 portrays schematically three such barriers. The first represents the protection of the body against the energies of the environment. Only where sense organs exist to encode the potential information can commerce occur between the environment and the organism. The second barrier bars access to immediate apprehension of information processed in the past. What evolutionary selection has kept as part of the innate informational store, of course, is always available when releasers occur. For

Barrier I	Barrier II	Barrier III	
Sense organ and perceptual thresholds	Evanescent immediate memory	Determined centripetal mnemonic ruts	
environment *(Neutral)*	**theater of perception** *(Degrees of Consciousness)*	**apperceptive mass** *(Unconscious)*	**perceptual future** *(Conscious Projection)*
Information as relation among physical energies, forms	Information from cognizing emotional reactions to feedbacks from other three regions	Information in memory whorls, innate and experience-produced	Information from new perspectives of projecscan centrifugal scanning
	* * * Interaction of all information with needs ↓ To motorium		

Table 2. Three Barriers to Availability of Information

previously acquired information, however, only a dual process can make possible the desired result. First, a retrieval set must save the information to establish a memory whorl in the Apperceptive Mass, and then at a later time of need a suitable retrieval cue reestablishes the set to redevelop the potential information in the whorl. The third barrier stops searching for new alternatives, which by their very definition have not been experienced and are not yet determined. The endeavor remains seemingly impossible as long as one thinks literally. But with the reperceptions from the perspective of the Perceptual Future of combinations of the familiar

111

memory whorls and of the environment, the difficulties lessen, and the new alternative becomes more probable. The skill of reperception uses a centrifugal scanning search that activates a train of memory whorls and resists being sucked into the regular retrieval ruts. Without conscious attention to the projection into the Perceptual Future, the forces are all in the direction of literal retrieval.

The Problem of New Alternatives

Although short-term memory and long-term memory satisfy the needs for information for most situations in a stable culture, they are inadequate for a changing environment in which the organism must seek further for new ideas to solve unaccustomed problems. Historically, remedy has been sought in formal discipline, transfer, and free association. Formal discipline crumbled under logical criticism and Thorndike's experiments. Transfer in all its forms including mediation has been shown to have negligible effect on new learning and problems. Transfer seldom helps more than does intelligently selective memory. Probably most surprising has been the determination that free association is extremely limited in its ability to arrive at new ideas. It concentrates either in pedestrian communities of response or in the equally limited experiential and emotional association of the individual which may have significance for his psychiatrist but holds no key to a fresh idea. The persistence of this limited community of response was examined after a quarter century on a similar college population by Russell and Jenkins (1954). More recently, hopes for real novelty from free association were raised again by the forcing procedures of Osborn and De Bono and by the operant shaping for originality by Maltzman. However, critical experiments by others and analyses according to the theory of this study indicate that the responses are superficial and occur largely in the peripheral regions of specific memory whorls and therefore miss creative alternatives. Even if one had a large computer to give the almost infinite number of combinations and permutations of associations, the problem of picking out the one which is relevant for the problem at hand would remain, because relevance has little to do with proportional identities. For creative transfer free association is not enough.

Since neither perseveration nor chance produces adequate new alternatives, anticipation seems the only other direction. Anticipation from the future presupposes projection as the first half of the cybernetic cycle. Euclid showed how differently a problem can be perceived when put into a new context. For instance, when the sides of a triangle are extended and a line parallel to one of the sides is drawn through the opposite intersection, how easy it then is to see that the sum of the angles of a triangle is half a circle or 180°. Freedom from the perceptual constraints of the original problem allows new associations. Avoiding the retrieval ruts represents an ever present danger for creative transfer. Most important is the way projection-anticipation maintains the relevance of the associations as genuine alternatives. Because it is the problem that is projected into the Perceptual Future, the needed context is never lost. An interesting example occurred during the planning for landing a man on the moon. Getting him there had begun to seem feasible, but how to get him off the moon again still remained a puzzle. Finally the LEM was reperceived not only as a landing craft but as a stand from which the capsule could propel itself into lunar orbit.

The ability for projection-anticipation probably arose from the eye's engagement from birth in distance reception. The saccadic eye movement darts from object to object in the environment as movement or some other factor draws attention involuntarily to it. These are the same movements, however, which a few years after birth have been disciplined to read a line of print in three jumps without regressions. The child's early inability to distinguish between his afterimages and fantasies on the one hand and the objects of the physical environment on the other suggests that the same saccadic movements range the same limits of the Theater of Perception and the Apperceptive Mass as those focusing on environmental objects. When the movement can be disciplined so that the problem can be projected into the Apperceptive Mass in a spiraling centrifugal movement, creative transfer (projecscan) becomes possible. At the same time the centrifugal set has to activate many memory whorls in order to have something to survey and yet has to avoid the approximating centripetal attraction of the memory whorls. Similar to the way one changes position to get a new perspective in the external environment the scanning focuses on those parts of the Apperceptive Mass temporarily awakened from their usual unconsciousness. At first these perspectives probably occur only in such favorable places as among contiguous organized whorls. Later they may involve separated whorls or even those between whorls in the Apperceptive Mass and an organization in the environment.

Just as the feedbacks from the environment and the Apperceptive Mass have their cognizing associated with relief from uncertainty and with the feeling of familiarity, the feedback from the projections into the Perceptual Future has its distinctive emotional tone too. The information in a relevant new alternative evokes a feeling of surprise—the Eureka explosion of Archimedes.

Unless the insight is "captured" by some sort of retrieval cue and is made a part of the Apperceptive Mass, its existence is as short as the immediate apprehension of information from the environment. Some sort of categorization, naming, and relating must occur to provide enough time to examine the new alternative thoroughly. Without a retrieval cue the new alternative soon becomes as elusive as the good idea in a dream or the bon mot in the midst of a conversation. The retrieval cue for the insightful perception adjusts the limen so that the alternative is discriminable and available at will.

The part of the Apperceptive Mass derived from the projecscan feedbacks seems to have a property not shared by ordinary memories. Its information evokes additional reperceptions, new perspectives and relations, and in some way invites further projections into this area. A person practicing creative transfer often produces new alternatives for a wide variety of problems.

One of the most important kinds of conscious management of behavior projects a goal into the Perceptual Future from where the attained goal is reperceived as a subgoal. This maneuver not only prevents the finality and closure from an attained goal but also makes possible more creative transfer through anticipations from the projected goal.

An Example

The house was to be built on a concrete slab on a little hill of solid granite. The city required that the waterline and the sewer line had to be in separate trenches five feet deep and ten feet apart. Estimated costs for blasting the two long trenches threatened to make the building venture untenable. While the thin soil was being removed to bare the rock for the slab and foundation footings, the thought occurred, "Why not lay the pipes on the bare granite and then use this dirt to make a hillock over them five feet thick?" At that moment flashed a memory of how some college trustees had satisfied the requirements of a benefactor's eccentric will that a very high wall be built around the campus. In their attempt to keep the school from looking like a prison they sought relief in vain from the courts. Then someone had the insight that the will had specified the height of the wall but had not stated that the wall had to be above ground. Projecscan theory can account for the new alternative for meeting the legal requirement without the expensive blasting. Where to place the earth to be removed from the foundation and how the pipes were to be buried the required depth were reperceived without the granite as an impediment. Whether the myth about the college wall was an after-association or whether it was included in the perspective for the projecscan, I am not sure. The incident illustrates, however, how tangential may be the associational elements in the solution of a problem.

Interpreting after-learning perceptually in terms of information seeking and processing within the Theater of Perception integrates a great diversity of topics in the psychology of learning. Assuming an active organism as the center, one avoids the puppet-dilemma posed for those who postulate the push from stimuli in the environment. The new model also permits development of consciousness as an emergent level of attention which is not a mere registrant, but plays an essential role saving processed information as memories or projecting problems into the Perceptual Future to search for new alternatives.

The theory postulated here outlines how from memories incapable of anything new, reperceptions for fresh approaches may follow the perspective of old memories from the Perceptual Future. The reiterated differentiation of projecscan (creative transfer) from literal transfer and memory is the underlying theme of this and the other chapters and opens the way to the practical deductions of the complete theory in chapter XIII.

Konorski (1963) closed his invited address to the Seventeenth International Congress of Psychology with these words, "the question of the 'whereabouts' crowning the given research should be reasonably asked only when the questions of the 'how' and 'why' have been already answered."

XII EXPLANATIONS USING THE PERCEPTUAL THEORY OF AFTER-LEARNING

*Theories are formulated to
account for phenomena.*
H. Leibowitz

A number of issues look very different from the point of view of the new perceptual theory. Some empirical results, apparently inconsistent, can now be understood, e.g., why principles sometimes do and sometimes do not aid creative transfer in a new situation. The theory also simplifies theoretical assumptions which have made such a puzzle of similarity as a factor in transfer. Finally, the embarrassment about the role of attention and consciousness in creative transfer need no longer obstruct a comprehensive theory and practice of after-learning.

The literature on Judd's concepts is equivocal on how successfully they have been applied in new situations. His *Education of the Higher Mental Processes* explained that principles had to be understood and learned in appropriate ways but did not specify those ways. Because principles are not homogeneous in structure, some may be no more than generalizations that the student has learned as facts. Even where one has the common elements of several discrete memories, e.g., the overlap of the fanlike retrieval loops between the Apperceptive Mass and the Theater of Perception in Figure 5, the device is an aid more to exact redintegration than to discovering new relationships. Not uncommon is the student who can work out a problem if someone first tells him what principle or formula to use.

The methods conventionally employed to transmit the structure of a principle can give no assurance of its application in finding new alternatives. For the last decade or more the plausible hypothesis that deriving a principle promises more transfer than being given the principle has been supported, however, by only as many experiments as the opposite hypothesis. That both deriving and given groups transfer more than their controls shows that a factor other than the derived-given continuum was operating. Some like Hendrix (1950) and the University of Illinois Mathematics Group contend that a principle loses much of its capacity to transfer when verbalized. They proscribe more than premature verbalization. Apparently, principles do not transfer unless a favorable perceptual condition exists.

The perceptual theory proposed here demonstrates why organization based on memory can give no more than a literal transfer while an organization based on projecscan has a much higher probability of novel alternatives. The paradox of deriving something new from the old depends on the reperception of the old memory organizations from the perspectives of a spiraling, centrifugal set in the free regions of the Perceptual Future. In contrast, the centripetal movement in a memory whorl favors exact memory. Moreover, the retrieval sets which save the new alternatives from quick disappearance seem to possess a growing edge that makes for additional projecscan around them.

Compared with the fragmentary and even artificial kinds of responses from various schemes for free association, the new alternatives from projecscan always retain a relevance to the problem. That should not be surprising because it is the problem, which is projected, around which a net of context develops in the Perceptual Future as it would anywhere else. The difference involves a sensitivity to the relations and implications of an organization. The person who has learned a generalization too literally seems incapable of applying it when the circumstance differs slightly. An interesting case of this was reported some years ago when the president of the United States gave orders not to say anything about a certain country until after its elections. A military censor passed congressional military committee testimony which from a strictly military context breached no security. However, because the dispatch did not contain the specific name of the country, the military censor missed how upsetting it could be when interpreted by that country in the context of the nearing elections (Pearson, 1963). This example suggests how even well-organized original learning, in order to be applied intelligently, must occur in a context of creative perception.

Another problem concerns memory. While emphasizing the indispensable value of projecscan in obtaining new alternatives, one must note that the new is derived from reperceiving combinations of memory whorls. Without development of a quantum of memory whorls, the projecscan process cannot even begin. Harlow found this true in baby monkeys, and human experience shows that originality cannot be created in a vacuum: The person who knows nothing about weightlessness will probably have nothing worthwhile to suggest on equipment for space flight. Therefore, the perceptual theory would consider memory necessary but insufficient for new alternatives.

The theory of after-learning offered in this study illumines several special topics related to memory. Stereotypy, for example, not only seeks no new alternatives but restricts response nonadaptively. This lack of differentiation implies that the normal process of seeking information (focusing and cognizing) has broken down. Pavlov reported such cases among his dogs as experimental neurosis. All conditioning was lost when too fine a line was drawn between excitation and inhibition. The new theory recognizes the intimate relation between needs and information. Under traumatic conditions an overwhelming emotionalized need, completely monotypic, forgoes information and automatically rushes toward the motorium.

Another curiosity in the field of memory is reminiscence. That better memory exhibited later over what can be produced immediately after reaching the desired criterion has usually been explained as the result of removal of inhibiting factors, particularly those in poorly organized materials. The new theory interprets such factors as inherent in the centripetal character of the memory whorl's plausible after-reverberations toward the node if there are no interferences.

Interferences of ready recall have been ascribed to retroactive and proactive inhibition because of similarities and other problems in the material, to changes of set, and to emotional factors. The new theory puts motivational and their associated emotional needs at the center of its model. Traumatic emotional experiences can inhibit relevant memories and accentuate others. Emotions also provide in the cognizing situation the basis for the continuance of information seeking from the Theater of Perception. Since the establishment of an appropriate retrieval set is essential for saving processed information in immediate apprehension, anything that confuses or bypasses that set will prevent correct recall. The way the new theory conceptualizes similarity and its relation to recall is dealt with in a latter part of this chapter.

The conventional behavioral explanation of insight learning as just a special case of fast trial-and-error learning (Mowrer, 1960) has difficulty explaining why insightful learning often shows good application to quite new situations and at least avoids the regressions and forgetting of its own problem. Projecscan theory offers a rationale that clarifies the issue between the Behaviorists and Gestaltists.

Since insight is a reperception of the means-goal relationship, the discrimination of the essential cue allows a quick retrieval over a wide range while a trial-and-error solution gets restricted to a specific reaction with erroneous stimulus generalizations on each side of the continuum from the problem. Thorndike's cats in the problem box clawed the empty air where the loop to pull open the lock had been located before its removal to another location in the box, and the animals took much trial and error to learn the new location. Adams, repeating Thorndike's experiment but placing the means and the goal of the opening door in such a way that they could be perceived together, found that the cats adapted quickly and "intelligently" to any change in the location of the means (Adams, 1929).

When a subject perceives anew a problem projected into the Perceptual Future and then actualizes it, he has demonstrated two important skills for further problem solving: How to reperceive from projecting and how to "save" the new alternative by prompt attention to a retrieval set for it. Sultan, Köhler's most insightful chimpanzee, extended his success with one kind of problem by rather abbreviated trials in a quite different kind, e.g., from piling up boxes to reach a lure to a type of pole vaulting. The permanence, i.e., freedom from subsequent saw-toothed regressions of time or errors, of projecscan solutions follows from the perception of the essential relationship for retrieval and application. Without insight, the retrieval is as apt to hit the outside of a whorl as its vortex, or even miss the memory entirely. What is commonly regarded as good learning of the rote variety may actually preclude projecscan since the retrieval loop is made so narrow and overdetermined that no response can be obtained when the situational cue is slightly different. The new perceptual theory thus controverts the assumption that insightful reperceptions can be subsumed under conditioning or trial and error.

Similarity has continued to be a crucial problem in after-learning. For retrieval, one view holds that the incoming stimulus representation is matched to some remembered cue and that transfer ensues according to the degree of similiarity. Projecscan theory, on the other hand, finds no need for the complicated matching but considers similarity a post hoc reaction when the individual feels his behavior is familiar. Then a self-conscious effort may allow him to trace and perceive likenesses in the older and present stimulating situations. At times, though, the feeling of familiarity may not reach the level that permits easy verbalization of the principle uniting the two situations (Heidbreder, 1948), even when the performance is really excellent. William James in his 1890 book first stated the general view about similarity which I have adopted. Noble (1961) proposed that similarity offers a criterion of transfer. The perceptual theory concedes this to be true only for literal transfer; for creative transfer (projecscan), as in the poet's figures of speech, the relation may be so tangential that a logical similarity criterion would be absurd. The theory rejects the hypothesis that a perception of similarity precedes or aids the retrieval of a memory.

Until perceived as such, a new situation may be objectively coincident and yet not be cognized as similar. The problem may often resemble the geometer's triangles that have to be placed in a certain way to test their congruence. More commonly, a certain context may prevent easy discrimination of similarity because of embeddedness (Duncker, 1945). An interesting example can be found in Kuo's kittens which spared and even fondled rats and mice they had grown up with but chased and killed strange ones (Kuo, 1938). From chimpanzee behavior I recall a mature male, Pan, who was indifferent or blind to the pumpkins growing in his large outside enclosure at the Yerkes Laboratory in Florida, but who destructively threw and smashed similar pumpkins introduced from the outside.

Although even extreme Behaviorists grant that only that part of objective stimulus objects attended to actually serves as a stimulus, attention and consciousness play no role in most learning theory. The perceptual theory of after-learning, on the contrary, finds these constructs necessary to understand how the resources of past and future perception and learning can become available out of the unconsciousness of the Apperceptive Mass.

The needs for information tend to concentrate at some point on the periphery of the Theater of Perception, toward either the external environment or the covert, unconscious world of the Apperceptive Mass. Several pseudopodia of an amoeba may be actively extended simultaneously, but only one point of attention can occur at a time in the Theater of Perception. Webster and Haslerud (1964) found that college students exhibited deterioration of the absolute limits of peripheral discrimination when attending to a central visual or auditory counting task. This kind of study helps us understand why one can pay attention to only one thing at a time. The forays in search of information focus on a figure against the general ground of the environment, or analogously, on a node in the Apperceptive Mass. Then follows the feedback into the Theater of Perception, interaction with the initiating need, and the cognizing phenomenon. The minimal degree of seeking can be identified with passive attention, the more intense voluntary and controlled active attention with consciousness. The search also can encompass only a limited number of discrete items (7 ± 2 in the adult).

When the information available in the external environment proves insufficient, attention turns to the Apperceptive Mass. To cash such a check, at some previous occasion a low order of consciousness must have saved, by an intent-to-retrieve, processed information from being extinguished in transit from immediate apprehension to the motorium. When new alternatives are imperative, high-level consciousness can project the problem into the Perceptual Future and reperceive attained goals as subgoals. With this control of one's own motivation, one can begin to speak meaningfully of a novel emergent, a conscious ego.

Some fail to distinguish between perceiving and actualizing. From the Gestalt and psychoanalytic literature one gets the impression that if insight somehow can be attained, the problem is over. However, Köhler's apes proved such poor engineers that their towers of boxes often toppled before they could climb up to the suspended lure. Likewise, the clinical patient needs a good deal of help to put his new understanding into practice.

The perceptual theory recognizes that insight is only a first step to creativity or some practical end; three additional activities must be undertaken before the desired goal can be reached. First, the evanescing insight must have its brief life lengthened by making it a memory whorl in the Apperceptive Mass. Second, it must be examined for logic and relevance. Third, materializing skills must support the whole project; otherwise it will fail. Such differing cases as the language to communicate, the mathematical background to prove a theorem, and the expertness on the potting wheel to bring into being a conceived form indicate the range of skills required to objectify a particular insight.

Perhaps enough issues have been sampled to show that the

perceptual theory of after-learning allows a rethinking of many topics. Other questions that might have been brought into the survey are as follows: how much later retrieval and projecscan are determined by sets at the time of original learning; how much the future can influence behavior; the relation of frequency to availability; the social and individual factors in creative transfer; and the evaluative process.

XIII EDUCATIONAL DEDUCTIONS

. . . a theory is the most
practical thing you can have.
J. S. Bruner

&S Earlier in this century psychologists like Thorndike, Judd, and
Dewey did not hesitate to spell out the educational implications of their theories and experiments. At a symposium held in
1959, however, Dr. Kenneth Spence, overwhelmed by its complex-
ity of factors and difficulty in experimental control, stated that the
psychology of learning at its present immature stage had nothing
to contribute to education. Dr. Underwood, although recognizing
how different laboratory subjects are from classroom learners,
concluded that some factors like meaningfulness, intertask and
intratask similarity, and active recitation as contrasted with passive
study had improved acquisition rate in the laboratory so much that
they might hopefully be applied to the classroom. The old problems of massed versus distributed and whole versus part learning
he would not include in the recommended list. As an empirical,
nontheoretical psychologist, he put forth the above as the best
conclusions of the Functionalists.

The question naturally arises what the present perceptual theory
of after-learning can offer as suggestions (subject, of course, to
prior critical testing in Regional Learning Centers) to the classroom. Both traditional and so-called progressive education have
neglected transfer and have not paid enough attention to the

future. For a dynamic society the future may be as imperative a frame of reference as aiming ahead of the duck to hit it in flight is for the hunter.

In order to develop a theory for the appearance of new alternatives it became necessary to rebuild the foundation for all after-learning on a perceptual base. The previously artificial segregation of the problem into sensation, perception, cognition, thinking, problem solving, imagination, learning, memory, transfer, and creativity has prevented that integration which can help the schools to understand learning and to encourage it in their pupils. An adequate theory of after-learning has implications for education at every level—from kindergarten to college to continuing adult learning.

When the whole after-learning process is fitted to a perceptual model, a Copernican simplicity supplants the previous complicated and sometimes conflicting systems and parts. To perceive is to discriminate differences in relationships; with such information the organism tries to satisfy its needs from hunger to curiosity. When the immediate stimulation does not present enough information, the search changes to the Apperceptive Mass and the Perceptual Future.

The full range of information is available only to those equipped with three fundamental skills. The student must learn to attend and discriminate; he must learn to establish the cues without interferences and then how to employ these in retrieval; finally, he must learn how to project into the Perceptual Future to find new alternatives. Primitive man emphasized the first kind of strategy because his was a here-and-now world. Civilization brought accretions of knowledge stored in memory and in writing. Even recent societies have depended on the sporadic inventor to solve its emergencies with a new idea and then often enough stoned the innovator. The encouragement of creativeness is only now gradually being recognized as a social necessity in a rapidly changing world. Moreover, encyclopedias and computer memories have diminished the need for retrieval from only a personal store.

Even today, for many situations, maybe as many as half, the first strategy is sufficient and because it is fundamental to the other two, it ought to be stressed in the early years and in the first schooling of the child. Unless he learns to avoid distraction and to hold attention for several seconds, the retrieval and projecscan skills cannot be developed. To detect differences in relations between stimuli is the basic skill for adjusting to the environment and also for developing the higher cognitive functions. Montessori recognized this many years ago. The basic learning skill is to control attention. In Skinner's *Walden Two* the children right from the start underwent trials to develop their attention and frustration tolerance.

Learning to reperceive for more insightful information from the external world can begin after the basic orientation has been established. Schiller (1952) found that young chimpanzees were unable to solve problems requiring insight about relations between objects in plain view. A year or two later with more maturity most of them could, especially if they could change positions and look at the problem from different perspectives. The practice and example of insights from immediate apperception can help the transition to the similar saccadic-like centrifugal loops in projecscan among the memory whorls of the Apperceptive Mass.

The establishment of the Apperceptive Mass precedes birth. A range of unlearned reactions have been identified with rather specific arousal stimuli. The development of retrieval cues to reinitiate response relations which had ceased to manifest themselves after a delay adds an ever increasing store to the Apperceptive Mass. To learn how to retrieve efficiently should begin in early years with delay of response experiences and proceed to more complicated types of memory.

The young child loves rote memorization and does it well, even when it involves the alliterations in nonsense nursery rhymes. However, since useful memory depends on relationships, as rapidly as motivation permits, the Apperceptive Mass should be accumulating meaningful materials. The organization of these by interrelated feedbacks makes the retrieval system surer through multiple cues. Experience in redintegrating from one part of such organized knowledge can begin early and develop competence in the second strategy (establishing cues without interferences and employing them in retrieval).

Special care to avoid interferences during the development of the retrieval cue improves the probability of its accurate redintegration. Ability in managing to have only something dissimilar follow on the heels of the learning and no incomplete or not well-understood materials learned in close succession will help. Short-term control to relax emotional blockages may be one of the best skills the child can learn. This can be accomplished essentially by concentrating attention on something—anything—e.g., giving undivided attention to the pressure your thumb is exerting against your index finger. Emotions are short-lived unless constantly strengthened by feedback from the disturbed organism.

When memory is examined for its place in a perceptual theory of after-learning, one can see how memory whorls in the Apperceptive Mass are basic not only for the categorization that extends immediate apprehension and for the retrieval of information on routine problems but also for projecscan. Efficient methods of establishing a retrieval set during original learning so that, with an adequate cue, the item or relation can be reconstructed include the following: good discrimination and identification; optimal motivation; attention to the relatedness or meaningfulness of the material; spaced study and review; and especially the intent-to-retrieve, a variant of the Zeigarnik effect. Understanding that memory is a centripetal process should help both the establishment of the intent-to-retrieve and the retrieval itself.

Most important should be the overlearning (learning beyond the point of mere recognition) of library and other social retrieval skills. How to read efficiently for information, how to use reference books, how to write a computer program, and how to retrieve and interpret material stored in a computer ought to be among the abilities of a modern educated person.

The third strategy—that of projecting into the Perceptual Future to find new alternatives—is the one not yet taught to any considerable degree in schools. Small children are poor transferers. Their main deterrents center on a preoccupation with the here-and-now of immediate apprehension and on their ignorance (an undeveloped Apperceptive Mass). What strikes an adult as humorous or clever in a child's response may not indicate understanding or the capacity to transfer the concept. For example, a three-year-old asked what a student is. After she was given a definition, she exclaimed, "Oh, students are people!" but then went on calling her doll a student because it had lost a leg.

Certain techniques to train the student in perceptual flexibility so that he can project his imagery to past and future as well as the present are as follows: Bring saccadic eye movements under control for scanning of imagery as well as a line of print. Develop an attitude of perceiving an attained goal as a subgoal and of projecting goals ahead, e.g., regarding graduation as a way-station on the road to further learning and a career. Encourage the search for new alternatives and hypotheses. Although this cognitive extending can be started early as part of the child's play and fantasy, by the time that abstractions can be employed by the child, the curriculum might well encourage hypothesis making and the working out of deductions and implications as part of the formal development of the third strategy.

The schools should recognize conventional "transfer" as really the inexact aspect of memory and therefore extremely unpromising as a source of new alternatives. For adequate development of creativity and application of learning the projective third strategy must be brought into the curriculum.

Programmed instruction in "teaching machines" or in specially printed books where a response has to be made to each small successive problem (a bit) before there is knowledge of results (reinforcement) has been promoted as the long-awaited panacea for educational ills. The students would receive individual tutoring from the machine and go at their own pace, and the teacher would be freed from routine to "teach." Where good programs have been written on the most indicated matter, e.g., elementary statistics, the method works well for many, though not all, students. However, after programmed instruction, students transfer creatively no better than those in more traditional learning situations. Some like Barlow (1961) and Galanter (1959) have tried to write programs that go beyond the material conditioned, but the results to date show little more than some literal stimulus generalization. Each of them has, however, recognized how the whole programming project fails in a fundamental sense if no creative transfer can be demonstrated. Since programming depends on the continuities of the retrieval pattern, the obstacles to getting beyond literal stimulus generalization transfer seem theoretically unsolvable. For the discontinuities of the projecscan leap to creative transfer not even a program made for each individual would suffice.

The student should be taught to increase his sensitivity to relevance in the cognizing function. Unless he differentiates the apt feedback from those not likely to be useful, little value will accrue to projecting problems into the Perceptual Future. Although cognizing is very personal, it can be sharpened by encouraging the reporting of feedback and followed by examining how closely it relates to the objective sought.

Many insights from projecscan are lost almost at once because like a gas balloon not held fast they vanish into the blue. The supportive skills of language not only aid communication but also help capture ideas. For example, an author may "see" that a character in his novel needs more capacity to accomplish the desired end, but only when the problem is put in words does the insight become workable. Before attempting a mathematical problem one may need to state what the problem is and what is already given. Not until a fuzzy hunch has been focused linguistically can a critical examination of it begin. The bright solution-provision of a Jungian dream needs a retrieval cue, written, spoken, or thought, to bring it back for consideration even a few minutes after waking. Hendrix (1950) warned against the premature stabilization of an idea in words, but some kind of retrieval cue must be employed if there is to be anything to consider. Research may indicate how to steer between these two extremes.

Most schools and colleges by their conventional examinations encourage memorization retrieval, restricted to the time of the examination. Longtime retention in the Apperceptive Mass and especially the kind of learning for later application and projecscan are thus indirectly discouraged. The usual multiple-choice examination (even those made from the question files provided by the textbook writers for the elementary course in psychology) seldom asks for more than straight recall, very often of those terms or names italicized in the text. Likewise many essay examinations require no creative transfer. Contrast what the effect would be on the kind of preparation if the student were told he would have to apply the facts that he would have to recall or that might even be given to him along with the questions. Overlapping examinations to reconsider and use material from earlier examinations in a course is one way to help create the proper set. In addition, if a department built advanced courses and their examinations on what was supposed to be learned in prerequisite courses as well as on new material, then this concern for the integration of knowledge would impress students that the college was taking its objectives seriously. With an increase in creativity by projecscan on the part of many individuals a new urgency to teach retrieval and evaluative skills will occur. Formerly, when only the "truths" were taught, evaluative skills received little emphasis.

Adult education, except in such places as the Gruntvig schools in Denmark, has lacked a theory of its purpose and possibilities. In the United States it has consisted mostly of vocational courses to complete a degree, to improve the level of certification, or to retrain for a new job. Adult education, as the never-ending continuation of the educational process started in school, with emphasis on the meaning of life, understanding the world, and knowledge of self and others, has hardly begun. Increasingly important for both vocational and psychological reasons in a changing world, adult education needs projecscan to refresh the individual's Apperceptive Mass and to help him compensate for the physiological and psychological handicaps that accompany aging.

The adult suffers increasingly from a slowing rate of mental and physical activity, poor retrieval of recent events, and inability to resist masking or crowding of stimuli presented simultaneously or in quick succession. These perceptual defects can be compensated for by various strengths. The older person who uses his skill in the organization and development of meaningful contexts often counterbalances his loss of speed and immediate memory. His ever larger Apperceptive Mass can be kept available and a good locus for projecscan. Most important for this objective is maintenance of the Perceptual Future and a growing edge. Sorenson (1930) presented some experimental evidence that continued learning for adults (in this case, teachers taking summer school courses to maintain certification) can act as a partial preventive of the inability to learn. If adult education and extension courses concerned themselves more with creative transfer, the positive effects would be even more impressive.

The liberal arts college, whether separate or a part of a university, has floundered about for seventy years seeking a rationale to replace formal discipline which comfortably had selected both the curriculum and the explanation of the educational process. The classical studies had claimed to develop the mind; obviously only they could provide the desirable curriculum. Thorndike's research made rethinking the educational process imperative.

The colleges now "experiment" with survey courses in the humanities and the physical, biological, and social sciences, or attempt to calculate how much distribution of specific courses in the various areas will provide a liberal education before concentration in the major, or offer a "Life Studies" program where students participate in defining objectives for courses that deal with contemporary problems and in evaluating their own performance. The faculties hope the devices will help the students find meaning in the learning process and in their own lives.

The various innovations, each proposed as a way to "revitalize" college education, have had their day and have left faculty, students, or both disenchanted. The survey courses, for example, so very popular during the thirties and forties suffered eventually because faculty could not be found to teach them and the students increasingly complained that the courses provided only a meaningless smattering of information.

While colleges and their students want a good outcome from the four undergraduate years, neither pay much attention to the effectiveness of the means to attain this objective. An underlying neglect of integration and creative transfer (projecscan) makes little of what is learned "relevant" to personal and social problems. The apparent discreteness of courses within departments and between one department and another would not exist if students (and faculty) related all they learned to succeeding courses and ideas and transferred creatively back and forth between the old and new learning.

Instead of persisting in ways that have not sufficed or of frantically trying new fads, a reexamination of fundamentals would be more in order. The perceptual theory of after-learning can contribute toward a rational basis for educational objectives and procedures. If the limitations of discrete memories and literal transfer for confronting new courses and the problems of a changing world were really understood, then there might be more general appreciation of what ought to be done. Might there not be an outcry that the student develop retrieval and projecscan skills and practice them as his horizon is widened and his Apperceptive Mass is enriched by an integration of science, art, literature, and philosophy? Entirely on their own without instruction, apparently only a few students discover how to transfer creatively.

This new perceptual theory may lead to a time when the liberal arts colleges unapologetically can proclaim their high and socially necessary aim as learning, critical and appreciative, for both knowledge and values, that relevantly transfers to the future as well as to immediate concerns of the individual and society and that over a lifetime builds to an increasingly interrelated and meaningful whole. Creative transfer directed toward integration of all one is learning ought to be the least common denominator of all education.

Creative transfer could become more abundant if the schools utilized the pertinent instruction, example, and the kinds of examinations that go beyond memory. All courses become relevant when taught for and learned with an integrating projecscan.

133

A Practical Example

I shall conclude this chapter by spelling out in detail the implications of the perceptual theory of after-learning for application by an individual to systematic study. I can express this most clearly in the form of a letter to a young man who is about to enter college.

Congratulations on being accepted for college! I am glad you asked for suggestions on how to improve your study habits because many boys arrive in college less prepared in this important skill than a majority of the girls in their high school. The reason often is motivation. Since little or no learning occurs when one is not interested, the first essential is to study with desire. You want to take the initiative to find the interest and value for each subject within yourself. No subject is interesting in itself; it has interested learners. If you find yourself in a class that does not fire you with enthusiasm from the beginning, make the subject interesting by linking it to your own past or present strong interests and future ambitions. When you sit down to study and you cannot because of daydreaming, recognize this as a symptom of competing motives. Perhaps you can straighten them out yourself, but if the difficulty in maintaining attention is excessive, you may want to take advantage of the college counseling service. Although your fellow students may claim that no one can study well except in a quiet, well-lighted, regular place, learning can go on under much less optimal conditions, but you will be using extra energy fighting against distractions.

Since what you do not understand is many times harder to learn and remember than that which has meaning for you, relate each new learning to what you already know. A new term becomes familiar when you define it in your own words as well as those of the professor. If your foundation in some subject is poor, go back as far as necessary to rebuild step by step the sound substructure for the present task. For example, frustration from not understanding calculus ought to lead you to an intensive review of your high school mathematics. Understanding the long reading assignments is less apt to come easily if you plod through them sentence by sentence. Much better procedure would be a rapid skimming of the whole to get a general orientation and then read discriminatingly a second time. The important details can be recognized and learned faster and better that way.

Beware of cramming at the last minute. Learning is a growth

process that requires time for development. The student who crams will mix up his knowledge and forget rapidly. Rather, space your study, which means an initial and a review encounter with each assignment. Similarly, reviews for examinations should be spaced. Note that unless you plan reasonable, definite times for recreation and other nonacademic activities, the slight self-discipline required for spacing studies and reviews may not be sufficient. The crammer acts expediently because he never allotted time to study regularly. The same number of hours unwisely concentrated at the end could have been used much more efficiently along the way.

Everyone needs cues to recall information accurately. Perfect your note taking in lectures, organizing them so they show clearly the relation between ideas. Make them brief but not scrappy since you want them meaningful when they are "cold." Plan to correct and study your notes *as soon as possible after the lecture* because one forgets rapidly what is just barely learned. You can make the ideas from both lectures and texts your own by asking yourself questions about their relation to what you already know. Incidentally, anticipating the questions that the instructor may ask on the examinations is a most realistic preparation for both the examination and later use. This active study also helps to control daydreaming. Most forgetting results from cues getting mixed up with each other. Whenever ideas or words seem similar, one will need to examine each of them discriminatively and take extra precautions to organize each group of related facts so that they will not be confused with a slightly different group. The confusion is greatest when similar learning experiences follow each other closely in time.

When you get into the routine of managing your motivation, relating everything to make sense to you, spacing your study, and taking good notes, you will realize that learning is not difficult; the big problem is retrieval, i.e., how to keep your knowledge available when you need it. Since passing examinations is the immediate college hurdle, prepare yourself both intellectually and emotionally. In your study and review you get ready to apply your knowledge to new problems by anticipating them. Emotional preparation requires the development of the kind of confidence in yourself generated by good past study and unhurried review but also an attitude that the examination offers an opportunity and not a threat. The technique of taking examinations involves *following directions*, budgeting time, maintaining alertness without emotional tension, and the optimal method for each type of examina-

135

tion. For essays work from a brief outline based on your study of the interrelationships of the ideas; if you start with the apparently easiest question, the retrieval process will less probably block. For objective examinations, hurry through those items recognized or recalled immediately and then return to work on the others which may then seem easier after your "warm-up" on the task. If at any time you become nervous or experience an emotional blocking, you can bring yourself rapid relief by any kind of distracting *voluntary* effort, e.g., *attending closely* for a few seconds to your tracing of a thin small circle on the edge of your paper. Fear dies fast unless you keep resuscitating it with your tension.

You are canny enough to want to secure permanent values from your college years. To make your education effective for life you will need to perfect your skills in retrieving information, in transferring or making your learning go beyond the given, and in integrating your knowledge. To keep your knowledge available make periodic reviews and learn how to use the library to retrieve its socially stored knowledge as well as to find additional cues for your own. Since you will probably have to recognize and use your knowledge in a way different from original learning, project your learning always beyond the immediate examinations into your future. Regard each examination, course, even graduation, as successive subgoals; an attained final goal at any stage stultifies knowledge. As you relate your past studies and experiences with the present subject, anticipate how it may aid in understanding the next. Finally, keep a growing edge by library browsing and by intentional learning in order to keep functional contact between your former learning and a changing world.

XIV CRUCIAL QUESTIONS FOR THE THEORY

*Prove all things; hold fast
that which is good.*
I Thess. 5:21

No direct test could probably be made of the supraordinate theory stated in chapter XI as follows: "The perceptual processes operate from the Theater of Perception in the same manner upon both the external world of stimulus energies and the internal world of memory and its variants." However, questions can be posed and deductions tested from the twelve subhypotheses. Should critical evidence accumulate against any of the subhypotheses, the principal theory and its relation to the weak subhypothesis would have to be examined critically, though it might still stand like a pier that has lost only one of its piles.

The plan involves stating again each of the subhypotheses and then asking relevant questions that might serve to test it experimentally. The three constructs, Theater of Perception, Apperceptive Mass, and Perceptual Future, similarly will be defined, followed by questions that may help to designate more adequately the dimensions and characteristics of each. Finally, the growing edge of the principal theory will be examined to see to what other directions the perceptual point of view could be turned.

The Subhypotheses

A. In the Theater of Perception the needs of the organism initiate searches for information by cybernetic loops whose feedbacks interact with the needs, the whole process continuing until the needs are met.

1. Is there no information except that sought by the needs? (This problem of the direction of initiation could be crucial in deciding between the external environment and the perceptual processes.)

2. How are the cybernetic loops initiated and stopped?

3. How do the needs interact with the incoming information?

4. Is the organism especially ready for its own proprioceptive information compared to that from other sources?

B. The interacting process of need and of cognizing feedback which stops the searching process for information is attended by a distinguishable emotional condition.

1. Is the emotion or feeling the agent of the stopping?

2. Is the emotion or feeling an organismic signal for release to the motorium? Or for a change to other needs?

3. What agreement among subjects would there be on the kind of emotion or feeling experienced when adequate information is found?

4. How good is the discrimination between pairs of release from uncertainty, feeling of familiarity, and surprise?

5. What is the timing of the cognizing? Does it occur before, simultaneously with, or after the interaction with the needs? The experimental answer could be crucial for this theory's position on similarity and recognition.

6. Would the psychogalvanometer provide a subtle enough indicator of the emotional changes in cognizing?

7. How does attaining a goal stop both literal and creative transfer? Is it a closure on the memory whorl in the Apperceptive Mass, an inhibition of projection, or is the effect entirely by way of the cognizing reaction?

C. The search for information goes through the sequence from environment to Apperceptive Mass to Perceptual Future as the earlier provide insufficient information and as such devices as coding, retrieval, and projection-anticipation are mastered to enter the later stages.

1. Is the intent-to-retrieve the only bridge to memories in the Apperceptive Mass?

2. Is coding for information in the external environment dependent on simultaneous involvement of the Apperceptive Mass?

3. Would the progressive shifts occur in subjects differing in mastery of the devices?

4. Are the progessive shifts general in the population or are there large individual differences of bypassing earlier stages in favor of a favorite source, e.g., persons who would search a social memory like a library before examining the immediate external environment?

D. A conscious intent-to-retrieve can save as a retrieval set enough of an informative relation to allow later reconstruction of the specific memory if interferences from other information do not occur at or soon after the establishment of the retrieval set.

1. What is the relation between what is recallable in (a) fragmentation process during failing of immediate apprehension; (b) reconstruction process (as in Haslerud and Clark, 1957)?

2. What is the effect of interference at various stages of 1 (a) and (b)?

3. Is availability more related to prevention of interference than to institution of retrieval set and process?

4. What is the relation of various levels of conscious intent to amounts recalled in 1 (a) and (b)?

5. Does the retrieval cue establish the set to approximate, or is the process more direct?

6. Is the intent-to-retrieve like the Ebbinghaus bringing back to criterion level?

E. Each discrete memory nodal trace is the convergent point of a centripetal series of cybernetic loops from the Theater of Perception to the Apperceptive Mass and back again, an arrangement which makes possible literal transfer from the outer loops during the approximating retrieval.

1. What evidence in addition to Slamencka's supports discreteness of memory whorls?

2. What evidence is obtainable experimentally that the whorls are isolated from each other except as connected through the Theater of Perception?

3. Is literal transfer more than poor discrimination on the periphery of memory whorls?

4. Are the centripetal loops merely historical in the formation and in the retrieval of the memory, or can they be shown to be like magnetic lines of force or holographic interference patterns that have a continuing existence?

F. The discrete memory whorls of the Apperceptive Mass can be related and organized only through overlaps of ends of the cybernetic loops in the Theater of Perception.

1. What is the relation between recall of a simple memory whorl and recall of a concatenation through a single retrieval cue?

2. When a principle is given, is there a build up of the same kind of fanlike overlap of loops as in inductive integration?

3. Through the overlap organization of loops in the Theater of Perception can new aspects be differentiated or do these depend like other new alternatives on the perspectives of projecscan?

G. The search for new alternatives becomes possible when both sufficient development of Apperceptive Mass has occurred and sufficient conscious control allows escape from the ruts of literal retrieval by centrifugal projection of the search for information into the Perceptual Future. Through fresh perspectives from there of the Apperceptive Mass, of the environment, or of the combination of both, new alternatives are generated and fed back into the Theater of Perception.

1. Can evidence be found in projecscan for any other kind of set than the centrifugal?

2. When the advancing centrifugal spiral of projecscan starts retrieval sets operating for a number of memory whorls, does it avoid the centripetal pull of each because of its own momentum?

3. How much are the new alternatives from projecscan due to

the perspectives on two or more memory whorls or to the associated anticipations from the projected goal?

4. What differences obtain between free association and projecscan in the freedom of the Perceptual Future?

5. What differences are there between the projecscan process applied in the Apperceptive Mass and in the environment?

6. What is the relation of projecscan to maturation, intelligence, experience, and neural integrity?

7. Is the psychological problem of old age a problem of attention, the retrieval process, projecscan, or all three?

8. Would an examination of the early lives of Terman's historical geniuses show a more than average early self-discovery of projecscan?

9. How much of projecscan is a given talent, and how much is teachable at different general ability levels?

10. During the striving for new alternatives, what is the relation between relaxation, after effort, and fruitful projecscan?

11. Are the discontinuities of projecscan only apparent and the continuities just as traceable as those for retrieval?

H. The consciously controlled projection of problems and goals into the Perceptual Future and the perception of attained goals as subgoals allow control of the very needs which power the initiating perceptual processes.

1. With hypnotic control of the degree of consciousness, what would be the effect on projection of goal and change of attained goal to the status of subgoal?

2. Experimentally can one determine how and when the perceptual change from attained goal to subgoal takes place?

3. Experimentally can one show that the lowering of activity as a behavioral episode ends does not occur when the attained goal is reperceived as on the way to a new projection of a future goal?

4. How similar is projection of a goal to other projecscan?

5. How can one demonstrate experimentally that by manipulating the goals and subgoals one is modifying the needs and their relation to information?

I. The Apperceptive Mass eventually includes three regions

which yield information in an ascending order from a region of innate readiness and conditioned responses, to a region of memory whorls saved by retrieval sets, and, most pregnant of all, to a region where new alternatives from projecscan processes have been captured into retrievable memory whorls.

1. How analogous is the retrieval of past information to attention's breaching of the sensory barrier with lowering of threshold?

2. What is the relation of level of motivation to entry into the higher regions of information? Would the Yerkes-Dodson effect be exemplified?

3. Can the projecscan set be applied in any area of the Apperceptive Mass? Does it depend on initiation of the set during original learning, as is the case with retrieval?

4. Does the "distance" of the Perceptual Future make any difference in the productivity of a projecscan set?

5. Do overlearned memory whorls allow as many new perceptual perspectives for alternatives as do those whorls with partial or minimal meeting of criteria?

6. How could one experimentally test the availability after a time of projecscan insights that had and had not been anchored by a retrieval cue?

7. How much more amenable to further development of projecscan is that region of the Apperceptive Mass derived from projecscan than the region derived by the saving of processed information from the environment?

8. How could one scale availability of information in the three regions of the Apperceptive Mass and make an absolute and relative census per individual?

J. An overt, practical solution to a nonroutine problem of an organism requires not only perception of a new alternative but also an adequate level of motivation, skills, and opportunity.

1. What is the relation of motivation to the number of insights actualized?

2. How much is the judgmental process independent of memory and projecscan?

3. What is the relation of the new alternatives of projecscan to creativity? Is creativity just that which is socially valued?

4. Can a test be devised to indicate that an individual actually has perceived a new alternative if he lacks skill in communication or in applying it?

5. To what extent can one correlate increase in facilities and opportunities with increase in practical solutions to nonroutine problems?

K. With development of skill in projecscan's centrifugal scanning and correlative skill in "capturing" the new information into retrievable memory whorls, it becomes feasible to use projecscan in original learning in order to achieve a growing edge in learning, better control of motivation, more useful memory, and a readier creative transfer.

1. How general a skill is projecscan?

2. Does a growing edge only improve skill in projecscan or does it change the Apperceptive Mass too?

3. Are the sets for retrieval and projecscan so different that learning can employ only one at a time? Or does the combination of projecscan and the "capture" of the new perspective for the Apperceptive Mass now seem the ultimate sophisticated way to learn?

4. What is the relative effectiveness in producing new alternatives of guided and self-initiated projecscan?

5. Can "sensitivity to relevance" be developed as part of a more advanced projecscan to secure new alternatives of higher quality?

6. Can retrieval and projecscan be taught directly for use in original learning or must they be developed in after-learning first?

L. Although feedback from both the environment and the Apperceptive Mass are attended by some awareness, it is the ultrastimulating feedback from projecscan that leads to the emergence of an "ego," a condition favoring increased integration and control of all learning and after-learning.

1. Is there a continuity of attention and consciousness, or does consciousness occur only after a critical level of attention has been passed?

2. What is the relation between projecscan skill in projecting and reperceiving and increases in awareness of one's own behavior and skill in modifying it?

3. To what extent can the Western man develop his projecscan "ego" control to regulate and distribute his needs and goals in the interest of both a desirable covert and a desirable practical world? Although the oriental Zen self uses control to negate needs and desires, does it develop by similar perceptual skills?

4. For wisdom, what are the relative weights to be allotted to knowledge (in the Apperceptive Mass), projecscan, and judgmental skill?

The Constructs

The *Theater of Perception* is a construct regarding immediate apprehension as a region where all interactions occur among initiating needs, the searching loops for information into and back from the external environment and the Apperceptive Mass, and the efferent resultant toward the motorium.

1. How can one identify the locus and measure the strength of attention (and projection) outward from the Theater of Perception?

2. How can one identify the locus and measure the strength of the various feedbacks toward the Theater of Perception?

3. By what tests could one make certain that all perceptual activity occurs in the Theater of Perception and nowhere else?

4. How can one show that although the reference may be to past, present, or future, perceptual activity exists only in the immediate apprehension of present time?

5. By what demonstrations could it be ascertained whether all contexts and organizations of needs, searches for information, and feedbacks can be found only in the Theater of Perception?

6. What possibilities of delay, of time variations, of constancy are there in the resolution of the perceptual interactions as it rushes toward the motorium?

7. How could one measure the relative consciousness of the various outgo and feedback aspects of the cybernetic loops?

The *Apperceptive Mass* is a construct of three regions of unconscious readiness, consisting of innate propensities and the conditioning based on them; learned intents to specific recall of information from the environment and established by retrieval sets; and similar intents-to-recall but based on the creative alternatives of projecscan.

1. To what extent are learned accretions in the Apperceptive Mass based on the same kind of capacity as the innate readinesses and developed consciously by directing attention toward fashioning retrieval sets?

2. Is the intent-to-recall, the retrieval set, the only bridge between the Theater of Perception and the Apperceptive Mass?

3. How could one demonstrate that the centripetal set to retrieve specific information reinitiates the same memory whorl each time?

4. What lines of evidence would prove that memory whorls are discrete and have no connection with others in the Apperceptive Mass except where they overlap in the Theater of Perception?

5. How could one determine where the feedback from the Apperceptive Mass into the Theater of Perception becomes conscious?

6. What are the perceptual characteristics of the node and the memory whorl of which it is a part?

The *Perceptual Future* is a construct of the relationships among memory whorls, in the interstices of the Apperceptive Mass and outside the rut-like, centripetal path of a retrieval set in a single memory whorl, and is accessible only by projecscan.

1. Do the sense organs scan the Perceptual Future in the same way they do the external environment? This might be studied by eye movements, e.g., the rapid eye movements that have added to knowledge of the dream states.

2. Do the new alternatives come from the freedom to reperceive at the point of perspective in the Perceptual Future, or do they occur in the Theater of Perception as part of the feedback from the

145

focus of the perspective, or do they in both of the cases above depend on anticipations from projection of the problem and its goal?

3. By what means does the centrifugal spiral projection into the Perceptual Future keep contact with the centripetal memory whorls and yet maintain separation from them?

4. How can one distinguish free association with its continuities in the centripetal whorl from the Perceptual Future with its apparent discontinuity and accessibility only through projecscan?

5. What location of the Perceptual Future can be postulated other than the interstices between the discrete memory whorls or the conceptual space from where there are an infinite number of perspectives of the contents of the Apperceptive Mass and the external world?

Foundational Experiments

I early became impressed that even the white rat in a long rectilinear maze organizes its learning. The widespread use of a single T-maze or of very short two- or four-unit mazes had made impossible any manifestation of this tendency. I found that its organizational characteristics could be most clearly demonstrated by the rat with free units before, between, or after those prescribed with a certain pattern. It was easy to distinguish between an entrance gradient with a sharply concave gradient and a convex goal gradient. The presence of such gradients before and after a subgoal (Haslerud, 1949) was made possible by adjusting the delay of food at the goal ten seconds to accentuate the subgoal. With a single unit before the subgoal to the side opposite to the stabilized turns to the other side, like a figure against a ground, the anticipatory goal type of gradient appeared in the preceding free units. After the subgoal, however, only a weak perseverative tendency for the pre-subgoal turn developed. When the end goal was not delayed but was at full strength, the pre-subgoal convex gradient continued but the post-subgoal perseverative tendency became so small that it looked like an entrance gradient. A 1957 study of mine examined what gradients would be observed when a six-unit single alternation pattern was preceded or succeeded by six free units or six single alternation prescribed units. When anticipated, the established pattern reached the criterion of four out of five trials in about 40 per cent of the trials necessary when the pattern could be perseverated. This was true for both the free and completely prescribed situations.

Using the strong convex anticipative goal gradient as an indicator, I ran a test of the rat's perception of the patterns required in the units preceding the goal (Haslerud, 1953). Apparently, on original learning naive rats do not distinguish between the mechanically blocked, no-error-possible kinds of turns and those required to avoid a cul-de-sac. After establishment of a pattern in the preceding free units, however, a change at the goal in cul-de-sac units immediately modifies the free ones, while the passive, forced turns leave the free units with the original pattern. With this differentiation of the effect of guidance on naive and experienced subjects, the conflicts in the earlier literature on guidance seemed to be resolved.

When human subjects were measured tachistoscopically by a new summation method at subthreshold exposures, the results indicated that anticipation of the last line of a limerick after becoming acquainted with the first four lines was significantly better than when no context was given (Haslerud, 1959). More interesting was the advantage in lower thresholds for relevant over irrelevant endings. This consistent lowering of threshold with even partial context showed that a seeking organism uses its attention and perceptual abilities appropriately.

Japanese and American sixth-grade children learned a list of nonsense symbols, each on a separate page and surrounded by eight symbols, two in each of the main compass directions. The Japanese children recognized primarily the symbols to the north and the Americans those to the west, as one might expect from the reading habits they had been taught. While approximating the focus on the central symbol, the subjects had also acquired incidental information most significantly in the direction of approach (Haslerud and Motoyoshi, 1961).

These several studies have been pointed out because they and others played a part in the evolution of the perceptual theory of after-learning. They show that even in the white rat sensitive indicators, like free units in a maze, can detect perceptual processes. In similar experiments with human subjects, anticipative and contextual characteristics of perceptual behavior have been easy to observe when the methods did not foreclose that behavior. Ideally, I should have experimented on supports for all twelve subhypotheses, but that will take more time than remains for me. My experiments have sampled here and there, but fundamentally this is a book of theory with most of it awaiting future tests.

Growing Edges

Although my perceptual theory concentrates on after-learning, subhypothesis K ventures into the field of learning. The perceptual point of view may have value for the simple as well as the rather sophisticated kind of learning in K. Especially the meaningful type of material might show differential economy according to the way the subject perceives the problem.

The discrimination between the possibilities of free association and projecscan may seem arbitrary. Obviously, more research is needed to define the boundaries and possible overlap.

In contrast to the unconsciousness of the Apperceptive Mass and of some reactions in the Theater of Perception, the theory emphasizes consciousness as crucial for institution of retrieval set, cognizing, and projecscan. The theory assumes that between whorls, nothing important occurs in the Apperceptive Mass. The assumptions of this theory may have excluded too much the influence of unconscious conditions on after-learning, but a quantum of conscious process in the Theater of Perception may be necessary in order to perceive at all and to manifest anything beyond blind physiology. Perhaps hypnosis and other depth techniques can test the above postulations.

The twelfth subhypothesis L introduces but does not develop very far the ego as an emergent. Once this higher level of perceptual capacity has been attained, an Allportian functional autonomy may largely supplant the physiological and cognitive needs that originally powered the perceptual processes.

XV EPILOGUE: WHAT EXPECTATIONS FOR MAN?

We know what we are, but know not what we may be.
Shakespeare

With a fresh start interpreting perceptually the phenomena of after-learning, I have proposed a theory that not only integrates the past knowledge in this field, but has growing edges as well. The theory allows specification of the conditions for creative transfer and identifies literal transfer as the blind alley it actually is. Basing the perceptual processes on the need for information to meet the physiological and cognitive requirements of the organism, the theory incorporates motivation into the system without being confounded by it. The theory satisfies the criterion of applicability too. It indicates why no significant projecscan is apt to be found with an impoverished Apperceptive Mass. It meets directly the concern of an educated person living in a time of change to keep his knowledge available and relevant.

What started as an integrative model of after-learning that would indicate where to place literal and creative transfer led to a reexamination of man and his potentialities. Man has changed from a here-and-now being to a creature whose behavior must also be influenced by information from his perceptual worlds of past and future. To reduce information for man to only that in the present environment, however differentiated by discrimination of invariants from learning, as does J. J. Gibson (1966), seems as much an oversimplification as John B. Watson's (1914) bypassing man's introspective capacities to make the same objective methods fit him as well as other animals.

Although information exists in the three worlds of past, present, and future, all activity and interrelations happen in the present time of immediate apprehension, the continuing function occurring within the Theater of Perception. This theoretical construct, whatever the physical location of its neurological correlate, acts as though a single region were the integrative center of the disparate kinds of after-learning and motivating needs of the organism.

The present model based on the Theater of Perception places man as the initiator and monitor of searches for information rather than as a puppet moved only by external forces. With the discovery of gating mechanisms in the reticular formation and of selective perception, it becomes increasingly improper for anyone to envisage man as the statue to which Condillac added various sense organs for the entry of appropriate stimuli. Man's needs, including the need to know which Pavlov called the "What is it?" reflex in his dogs and which Aristotle considered the distinguishing mark of man, initiate the searches for information to aid in solving the problems evidenced by the needs. Though the environmental energies may create problems for man as an organism, only those stimuli for which he has readiness become information. As J. J. Gibson has adequately supported, the sense organs serve the perceptual systems, and learning improves the discrimination of invariants in the environment.

What is returned as information in the cybernetic loop to the Theater of Perception is a relationship or pattern. The stimuli as environmental energies never get past the sense organs but are there changed into a neural and perceptual code that can be as readily responded to in the Theater of Perception as any Fortran message in a computer program. The returning information fits into a context of needs, information from various other sources, and responses. The dynamic center acts always as a whole because of its very construction.

The Theater of Perception should not be thought of as other

than the site of significant action; no ghostly players act and no drama unfolds. While no homunculus or "executive," to use Neisser's term, has been postulated in the perceptual theory, several consequences of the feedbacks from searches for information require postulation of activities which might be termed *attention* and *consciousness*. The Theater of Perception, instead of homogeneously distributing its energies, concentrates them here and there as the organism's needs change. Attention focusing behavior within a limited span signals the start and direction of a search for information. The cognizing activity within the Theater stops the search when the information provided by a feedback loop leads to a closure on the final-common-path to some kind of response. The emotional situations of familiarity, surprise, or reduction in uncertainty accompanying the closure are distinctive enough to be discriminative cues of the cycle itself. With the closure, attention shifts to other needs.

Consciousness might be considered epiphenomenal if it were merely the heightened intensity of activity in the Theater of Perception during times of prolonged and frustrating searches for appropriate information. However, intents-to-retrieve, which initiate the centripetal sets that save some events in immediate apprehension from oblivion, probably seldom occur without a modicum of conscious shift of energy. Even a higher level of consciousness is necessary to project searches for information as a centrifugal set for projecscan. Since it must safeguard against falling into an ordinary retrieval rut and also focus on several memory whorls at a time from an interstice apart from them, consciousness in the present model serves a directive, monitoring role. Sperry (1969) has described just such a function as an emergent property of cerebral activity. As in the nervous system with recurrent nerves, the perceptual feedback loops of the Theater of Perception make its own activity part of the stimulating situation.

Where primitive man faced a continuing scarcity of information and almost everything was unknown or only guessed at, we now are overwhelmed with information in periodicals and books that accumulates in geometric ratios. Religious and political fanatics burned libraries in the ancient world because of fear of what their books contained. Unhappily the modern world has had a Hitler and others who have felt impelled to destroy knowledge. But quite apart from the mad ones, many feel like the Sorcerer's Apprentice who sought to shut off the water. Actually, retrieval technology has kept up quite well with the improved reference guides, microfilm, and now the computer retrieval programs. The problems, however, outrun even the vast memory resources. Even the largest libraries and computers can only canvass what is and was known. To generate really new alternatives the search has to turn elsewhere.

A new kind of biological technique was developed by a few men who probably quite by accident learned to scan the isolated memory whorls of their Apperceptive Mass by the same kind of saccadic leaps and focuses that they used in surveying the environmental world for its informative invariances. The insights from reperceptions of relations in the world could be matched and exceeded by the new perspectives on the accumulated individual and social memories of the wide range of experiences no longer physically present. The trick was to reperceive without falling into pedestrian retrieval ruts. In fact, any distraction, loss of morale, or fatigue could reduce the concentration on the centrifugal search enough to result in a regression to plain memory retrieval. Projec-scan seems possible only when the organism's nervous system has matured sufficiently and when a quantum of retrievable Apperceptive Mass has been developed.

The weary, cynical writer of Ecclesiastes 1:9, who commented, "The thing that hath been, it is that which shall be; and that which is done is that which shall be done; and there is no new thing under the sun," saw only a world of literal transfer of identical elements and did not realize the infinite creative possibilities of man's perceptual processes. What can man's behavior become when he really comprehends how to live in and use the resources of the undetermined Perceptual Future? At least three profound changes seem credible.

First, he can be freed from the heavy hand of determinism of the past whose indelible writing by the "moving finger" oppressed

Omar Khayyam and many another. Likewise, the vagaries of Hobson's choices in the present may sometimes yield to a rational alternative if one has learned how to find it despite hopeless obstacles. Only perceptually in the undetermined future can one find freedom, the opportunity to choose a course of action. To accomplish this desirable end the future must be made perceptually real by regarding attained goals as subgoals and projecting ahead the problem at hand. Unless the individual finds ways to anticipate and prepare for the future perceptually, he is fated to bruise himself when he bumps into it.

Second, man can become more creative. With the wide individual differences, genetically and from experience, and the illimitable potential perspectives from each person's projecscanning, there seems no basis for denying anyone a great deal of latent originality. That is fortunate because the modern tempo of accelerated change requires for physical and psychological survival that all men become more creative. The problems come faster than does the recording of adequate information on how to deal with them from social retrieval resources. Happily, the conditions favorable to finding new alternatives, e.g., by projecscan, by relaxation after effort, by receptiveness to new perspectives, are all teachable. The new theory should reduce the anxiety of the artist that his well will go dry. To be sure, Lehman (1953) found in the lives of historically significant persons that their greatest work was produced in early maturity and that many just repeated their early themes afterward. While that may have been generally true in the past, it does not have to be true now. The new theory suggests that the artist does not have to depend on chance inspiration but through projecscan can have confidence that his growing Apperceptive Mass and the cultivation of his Perceptual Future will provide more new alternatives and ideas than he can actualize in a lifetime.

Nuttin (1963) has studied how much behavior has a future referent. He has also demonstrated experimentally how the behavioral future is manifested in the *open* task (one unfinished, as in learning). The connections he draws among the dynamic, cognitive, and learning factors, as expressed in such statements as "cog-

154

nitive functions are able to transform needs into future-oriented plans and tasks," seem consonant with the present perceptual theory of after-learning.

By defining intelligence as "the degree of availability of one's experiences for the solution of immediate problems and the anticipation of future ones," Goddard (1946) made us realize how intimate the relation is among past, present, and future aspects of learning and after-learning.

In a discussion at a symposium on the integration of individual and population life cycles, Parsons (1967) presented this evidence from human socialization: "The only basis on which it is possible for parents to produce acceptable adults in their children, is to produce a wish to be parents themselves in turn ... The whole thing is so set up that the contemporary functions cannot be performed without providing for the future functions."

With projecscan in the Perceptual Future man discovers a new world of freedom and perceptual space. The psychologist Viktor Frankl (1959) discovered in the terrible world of the Nazi death camp that "it is a peculiarity of man that he can only live by looking to the future ... " Though he was suffering from privation and sores on his feet, he could withstand the hardship by imagining how some day he would be lecturing about the psychology of the concentration camp. Instead of accepting the finality of the present and behavior as closed, projecting the problem into the future allows a reperception that may affect all aspects of a situation. For man harassed by an overcrowded world, perceptual space may be the only frontier left for him. Besides freedom, the infinite number of perspectives on the combinations of memory whorls in his Apperceptive Mass offer continuing interest as an antidote to ennui and boredom. The extent to which a person can remake the actual environment by perceptual means is well illustrated by the account of Edith Bone (1957). During seven years of solitary confinement in a communist prison in Budapest, she kept her ego whole and morale unbroken by creative transfer. She took imaginary walking tours in the cities she had known; she reviewed her knowledge; she solved mathematical problems on an abacus she made from bread crumbs.

Not suprisingly, the perceptual theory also has some ethical implications as a third potential dividend from the Perceptual Future. When a person can perceive alternatives from projecscan and can also consider each in terms of its future consequences, he is freed from expedience and may elect a more responsible course. If he has no alternative available, how can he be said to act morally, even if his behavior is within conventional expectations? This preexamination of alternatives can take the place of feelings of guilt over missed opportunities or impulsive, unwise behavior. It is obvious that projecscan can add new dimensions to moral maturity.

The proportion of man's potentialities that are realized hardly ever gets estimated at more than 10 per cent. Perhaps that figure can be doubled or quadrupled with additions to the social memory from the computer and with the widespread use of projecscan to help each person keep his knowledge alive and creative. Increasingly all men will have to share Norbert Wiener's concern about *The Human Use of Human Beings*.

On a library wall at Dartmouth College José Orozco painted a disturbing mural entitled "Gods of the Modern World." It is startling to find that these are skeletons in academic gowns. One of them is delivering from a skeleton in labor in a torrent of books an infant skeleton already capped academically with the familiar black square hat. This symbolic dead knowledge is then depicted as embalmed in jars and books! The precious social memory store and that in the Apperceptive Mass grow strange and incomprehensible, even moribund, when transferred merely literally. However, if creative transfer reperceives, knowledge is reborn to transmit intellectual life one generation further, until again it must be revivified by rediscovery.

REFERENCES AND INDEX

REFERENCES

Adams, D. K. Experimental studies of adaptive behavior in cats. *Comp. Psychol. Monogr.*, 1929, 6, No. 27, 1-168.

Allport, F. G. *Theories of perception and the concept of structure.* New York: John Wiley & Sons, 1955.

Allport, G. W. Eidetic imagery. *Brit. J. Psychol.*, 1924, 15, 99-120.

Alpert, A. The solving of problem-situations by preschool children. *Teachers College Columbia University Contributions to Education*, 1928, No. 323.

Army Research Office. *Problems guide*, 1961.

Asch, S. E. A reformulation of the problem of associations. *Amer. Psychol.*, 1969, 24, 92-102.

Barlow, J. A. Aspects of teaching machine programming: Learning and performance. *Psychol. Record*, 1961, 11, 43-46.

Bartlett, F. C. *Remembering.* Cambridge: Cambridge University Press, 1932.

Berlyne, D. E. Recent developments in Piaget's work. *Brit. J. educ. Psychol.*, 1957, 27, 1-12.

Bestor, A. *The restoration of learning.* New York: Alfred Knopf, 1955.

Birch, H. G. The relation of previous experience to insightful problem solving. *J. comp. Psychol.*, 1945, 38, 367-383.

Bone, E. *Seven years' solitary.* New York: Harcourt, Brace, 1957.

Boring, E. G. *The physical dimensions of consciousness.* New York: The Century Company, 1933.

Borsodi, R. *The definition of definition.* Boston: Porter Sargent Publisher, 1967.

Broadbent, D. E. Flow of information within the organism. *J. verb. Learn. verb. Behav.*, 1963, 2, 34-39.

Bronk, D. Evaluation of graduate work in natural sciences at land grant institutions. A lecture given at Kansas City, Missouri, November, 1961, at the Centennial Convocation of Land Grant Colleges and State Universities.

Brown, W. L., and J. E. Overall. Concept discrimination in rhesus monkeys. Report 58-35, January, 1958. Air University School of Aviation Medicine, USAF, Randolph AFB, Texas.

Bruner, J. S. *The process of education.* Cambridge, Mass.: Harvard University Press, 1960.

———. What social scientists say about having an idea. *Printer's Ink Magazine,* 1957, 260, 48–52.

———, J. Goodnow, and G. Austin. *A study of thinking.* New York: John Wiley & Sons, 1956.

Bruner, J. S., G. A. Miller, and C. Zimmerman. Discriminative skill and discriminative matching in perceptual recognition. *J. exp. Psychol.,* 1955, 49, 187–192.

Bugelski, B. R., and T. C. Cadwallader. A reappraisal of the transfer and retroactive surface. *J. exp. Psychol.,* 1956, 52, 360–366.

Burack, B., and D. Moos. Effect of knowing the principle basic to solution of a problem. *J. educ. Res.,* 1956, 50, 203–208.

Caron, A. J., S. M. Unger, and M. B. Parloff. A test of Maltzman's theory of originality training. *J. verb. Learn. verb. Behav.,* 1963, 1, 436–442.

Chamberlin, D., et al. *Did they succeed in college?* New York: Harper & Bros., 1942.

Conant, J. P. *Education and liberty—the role of schools in a modern democracy.* Cambridge, Mass.: Harvard University Press, 1957.

Coxe, W. W., Jr. The influence of Latin in the spelling of English words. *J. educ. Res.,* 1924, 9, 223–233.

Crossman, E. R. F. W. Information processes in human skill. Diagram reproduced in J. P. Guilford, *The nature of human intelligence.* New York: McGraw-Hill, 1967, p. 256.

Darwin, C. Autobiography. In F. Darwin, *The life and letters of Charles Darwin.* New York: Basic Books, 1959.

De Bono, E. *New think: The use of lateral thinking in the generation of new ideas.* New York: Basic Books, 1967.

Dement, W. C. An essay on dreams: The role of physiology in understanding their nature. In T. M. Newcomb (Ed.), *New directions in psychology.* Vol. II. New York: Holt, Rinehart & Winston, 1967.

Duncker, K. On problem-solving (Trans. L. S. Lees from the 1935 original). *Psychol. Monogr.,* 1945, 58, No. 5.

Elder, J. H. Personal communication, 1961.

English, H. B., and A. C. English. *A comprehensive dictionary of psychological and psychoanalytical terms.* New York: Longmans Green & Co., 1958.

Flanagan, J. C. (Ed.). *The aviation psychology program in the Army Air Forces.* AAF Aviation Psychology Program Research Report No. 1. Washington, D.C.: U.S. Government Printing Office, 1947.

Frankl, V. E. *From death camp to existentialism.* Boston: Beacon Press, 1959.

Freud, S. Beyond the pleasure principle. In J. Rickman (Ed.), *A general selection from the works of Sigmund Freud.* New York: Doubleday & Co., 1957.

Frisch, J. E. Research on primate behavior in Japan. *Amer. Anthrop.,* 1959, 61, 584–596.

Gaito, J. Stages of perception, unconscious processes, and information extraction. *J. gen. Psychol.,* 1964, 70, 183–197.

Galanter, E. H. (Ed.). *Automatic teaching: The state of the art.* New York: John Wiley & Sons, 1959.

Gentry, G., J. E. Overall, and W. L. Brown. Transposition of response to the intermediate-size stimulus in rhesus monkeys. Report No. 59-11, January, 1959. Air University School of Aviation Medicine, USAF, Randolph AFB, Texas.

Getzels, J. W. and P. O. Jackson. *Creativity and intelligence.* New York: John Wiley & Sons, 1962.

References

Gibson, E. J. *Principles of perceptual learning and development.* New York: Appleton-Century-Crofts, 1969.

Gibson, J. J. *The senses considered as perceptual systems.* Boston: Houghton Mifflin, 1966.

Goddard, H. H. What is intelligence? *J. soc. Psychol.,* 1946, 24, 51-69.

Guilford, J. P. The structure of intellect. *Psychol. Bull.,* 1956, 55, 267-293.

————. *The nature of intelligence.* New York: McGraw-Hill, 1967.

Haber, R. N. Effect of prior knowledge of the stimulus on word recognition processes. *J. exp. Psychol.,* 1965, 69, 282-286.

————, and R. B. Haber. Eidetic imagery. I: Frequency. *Perceptual and Motor Skills,* 1964, 19, 131-138.

Handlin, O. Live students and dead education. *Atlantic Monthly,* 1961 (September), 208, No. 3, 29-34.

Harlow, H. F. Learning set and error factor theory. In S. Koch (Ed.), *Psychology: A study of a science.* Vol. II. New York: McGraw-Hill, 1959.

Haslerud, G. M. A comparison of free and prescribed maze pattern of the rat. Ph.D. dissertation. University of Minnesota, Minneapolis, 1934.

————. Form and interaction of goal and entrance gradients in a linear maze. *J. of Psychol.,* 1945, 20, 249-257.

————. Properties of bi-directional gradients at subgoals. *J. genet. Psychol.,* 1949, 74, 3-16.

————. Anticipative transfer of mechanically guided turns. *J. exp. Psychol.,* 1953, 45, 431-436.

————. Behavioral supports for transfer. *Tohoku Psychologica Folia,* 1957, 15, Fasc. 1-2, 1-6.

————. Transfer from context by subthreshold summation. *J. educ. Psychol.,* 1959, 50, 254-258.

————. Teach anything to anyone at any age in some form. Review of J. S. Bruner, *The process of education. Comtemp. Psychol.,* 1961, 6, 356-357.

————. Relation between the way general and specific principles are learned and how they are used. Project 3108, Contract No. 5-0560-2-12-1, 1968 (ERIC, ED 019 710). Washington, D.C.: U.S. Dept. of Health, Education, and Welfare, Office of Education.

————, and R. E. Clark. On the redintegration of words. *Amer. J. Psychol.,* 1957, 70, 97-101.

Haslerud, G. M., and R. Motoyoshi. Direction of incidental learning in relation to Japanese and American reading habits. *Perceptual and Motor Skills,* 1961, 12, 142.

Hayes, K. J., and C. Hayes. Imitation in a home-raised chimpanzee. In A. J. Riopelle (Ed.), *Animal problem solving.* Baltimore: Penguin Books, 1967.

Heidbreder, E. The attainment of concepts. VI. Exploratory experiments on conceptualization at perceptual levels. *J. Psychol.,* 1948, 26, 193-216.

Held, R. Plasticity in sensory-motor systems. *Sc. Amer.,* 1965, 312, No. 5, 84-94.

Hellebrandt, F. A., and J. C. Waterland. Indirect learning. The influence of unimanual exercise on related muscle groups of the same and the opposite side. *Amer. J. phys. Med.,* 1962 (April) 41, 45-55. (Also personal communication.)

Helson, H. *Adaptation-level theory: An experimental and systematic approach to behavior.* London: Harper & Row, 1964.

Hendrickson, G., and W. Schroeder. Transfer of training in learning to hit a submerged target. *J. educ. Psychol.,* 1941, 32, 206-213.

Hendrix, G. Prerequisite to meaning. *Math. Teacher,* 1950, 43, 334-339.

Herrigl, E. *Zen in the art of archery* (Trans. R. F. C. Hull). New York: Pantheon Books, 1953.

Hilgard, E. R., and G. H. Bower. *Theories of learning* (3rd ed.). New York: Appleton-Century-Crofts, 1966.

Hilgard, E. R., R. D. Edgren, and R. R. Irvine. Errors in transfer following learning with understanding: Further studies with Katona's card-trick experiments. *J. exp. Psychol.*, 1954, 47, 457-464.

Hilgard, E. R., R. P. Irvine, and T. E. Whipple. Rote memory, understanding, and transfer: An extension of Katona's card-trick experiments. *J. exp. Psychol.*, 1953, 46, 288-292.

Hughes, H. S. Lecture on Oswald Spengler at University of New Hampshire, March 11, 1961.

Hull, C. L. Mind, mechanism, and adaptive behavior. *Psychol. Rev.*, 1937, 44, 1-32.

Humphreys, L. G. The effect of random alternation of reinforcement on the acquisition and extinction of conditioned eyelid reactions. *J. exp. Psychol.*, 1939, 25, 141-158.

Hutchinson, E. D. *How to think creatively.* New York: Abingdon Press, 1949.

Imanishi, K. Social behavior in Japanese monkeys, Macaca fuscata. *Psychologia,* 1957, 1, 447-54.

Jacobson, C. F., and G. M. Haslerud. Restitution of function after cortical lesions in monkeys. *Psychol. Bull.*, 1935, 32, 563-564.

James, W. *Principles of psychology.* New York: Henry Holt, 1890.

Jenkins, J. J. Mediated associations: Paradigms and situations. In C. N. Cofer and B. S. Musgrave, *Verbal behavior and learning.* New York: McGraw-Hill, 1963.

Johdai, K. A field theory of extinction and spontaneous recovery. *Psychol. Rev.*, 1956, 63, 243-248.

Judd, C. H. The relation of special training to general intelligence. *Educat. Rev.*, 1908, 36, 28-42.

―――. Autobiography. In Carl Murchison (Ed.), *History of psychology in autobiography.* Vol. II. Worcester, Mass.: Clark University Press, 1932.

―――. *Education as cultivation of the higher mental processes.* New York: Macmillan, 1936.

Katona, G. *Organizing and memorizing.* New York: Columbia University Press, 1940.

Kay, H. Address at last session of Nineteenth International Congress of Psychology, London, August 3, 1969.

Klüver, H. An experimental study of the eidetic type. *Genet. psychol. Monogr.*, 1926, 1, 71-230.

Koch, S. (Ed.). *Psychology: A study of a science.* Vol. I. New York: McGraw-Hill, 1959.

Koffka, K. *Principles of Gestalt psychology.* New York: Harcourt, Brace, 1935.

Köhler, W. *The mentality of apes* (Trans. E. Winter). New York: Harcourt, Brace, 1925.

―――. *Gestalt psychology.* New York: Mentor Book MT644, 1947.

Kolers, P. A. Interlingual facilitation of short-term memory. *J. verb. Learn. verb. Behav.*, 1966, 5, 314-319.

Konorski, J. On the mechanism of instrumental conditioning. *Proceedings of XVII International Congress of Psychology*, 1963, 45-59.

Korzybski, A. *Manhood of humanity* (2nd ed.). Lakewood, Conn.: International Non-Aristotelian Library Pub. Co., 1950.

Krechevsky, I. "Hypotheses" versus "chance" in the presolution period in sensory discrimination-learning. *University of California Publications in Psychology*, 1932, 6, 27-44.

Kuo, Z. Y. Further study of the behavior of the cat toward the rat. *J. comp. Psychol.*, 1938, 25, 1-8.

Lashley, K. S., and M. Wade. The Pavlovian theory of generalization. *Psychol. Rev.*, 1946, 53, 72-87.

Lawrence, D. H., and G. R. Coles. Accuracy of recognition with alternatives before and after the stimulus. *J. exp. Psychol.*, 1954, 47, 208-214.

Lehman, H. C. *Age and achievement.* Princeton, N.J.: Princeton University Press, 1953.

McAllister, W. G. A further study on the delayed reaction in the rat. *Comp. Psychol. Monogr.*, 1932, 8, No. 2, 1-103.

MacCorquodale, K. An analysis of certain cues in the delayed response. *J. comp. Psychol.*, 1947, 40, 239-253.

———, and P. E. Meehl. On a distinction between hypothetical constructs and intervening variables. *Psychol. Rev.*, 1948, 55, 95-107.

Maltzman, I. On the training of originality. *Psychol. Rev.*, 1960, 67, 229-242.

Marx, M. H. (Ed.). *Theories in comtemporary psychology.* New York: Macmillan, 1963.

Mednick, S. A. The associative basis of the creative process. In M. T. Mednick and S. A. Mednick (Eds.), *Research in personality.* New York: Holt, 1963, pp. 583-596.

Melton, A. W. Implications of short-term memory for a general theory of memory. *J. verb. Learn. verb. Behav.*, 1963, 2, 1-21.

Miller, G. A. The magical number seven, plus-or-minus two, or, some limits on our capacity for processing information. *Psychol. Rev.*, 1956, 63, 81-97.

———, and J. A. Selfridge. Verbal context and the recall of meaningful material. *Amer. J. Psychol.*, 1950, 63, 176-185.

Miller, G. A., E. Galanter, and K. H. Pribram. *Plans and the structure of behavior.* New York: Holt, 1960.

Miller, N. E., and J. C. Dollard. *Social learning and imitation.* New Haven: Yale University Press, 1941.

Morris, R. *The quality of learning.* London: Methuen, 1951.

Mowrer, O. H. *Learning theory and behavior.* New York: John Wiley & Sons, 1960.

Neisser, U. *Cognitive psychology.* New York: Appleton-Century-Crofts, 1967.

Noble, C. E. Meaningfulness (m) and transfer phenomena in serial verbal learning. *J. Psychol.*, 1961, 52, 201-210.

Norman, D. A. Toward a theory of memory and attention. *Psychol. Rev.*, 1968, 75, 522-536.

Nuttin, J. R. The future time perspective in human motivation and learning. *Proceedings of XVII International Congress of Psychology*, 1963, 60-82.

Olds, J. The central nervous system and the reinforcement of behavior. *Amer. Psychol.*, 1969, 24, 114-132.

Osborn, A. F. *Applied imagination.* New York: Scribner's, 1957.

Osgood, C. E. The similarity paradox in human learning: A resolution. *Psychol. Rev.*, 1949, 56, 132-143.

———. *Method and theory in experimental psychology.* New York: Oxford University Press, 1953.

Pace, C. R. *They went to college.* Minneapolis: University of Minnesota Press, 1941.

Parsons, T. Discussion in R. R. Grinker (Ed.), *Toward a unified theory of human behavior* (2nd ed.). New York: Basic Books, 1967.

Pavlov, I. The first sure steps along the path of a new investigation (Nobel Prize address December 12, 1904). In M. Kaplan (Ed.), *Essential works of Pavlov.* New York: Bantam Books, 1966.

Pearson, D. Washington Merry-Go-Round column. *Concord Monitor* (New Hampshire), April 6, 1963.

Peterson, J. The effect of attitude on immediate and delayed reproduction: A class experiment. *J. educ. Psychol.,* 1916, 7, 523-532.

Peterson, L. R., and M. J. Peterson. Short-term retention of individual verbal items. *J. exp. Psychol.,* 1959, 58, 193-198.

Picasso, P. *Forty-nine lithographs.* New York: Lear Publishers, 1947.

Plato. *The republic* (Trans. J. L. Davis and D. J. Vaughn). New York: The Nottingham Society (circa 1914).

Polya, G. *How to solve it.* Princeton, N.J.: Princeton University Press, 1945.

Postman, L., and J. S. Bruner. The perception of error. *Brit. J. Psychol.,* 1951, 42, 1-10.

Postman, L., and D. L. Postman. Change in set as a determinant of retroactive inhibition. *Amer. J. Psychol.,* 1948, 61, 236-242.

Pressey, S. C., and J. E. Janney. *Casebook of research in educational psychology.* New York: Harper & Bros., 1937.

Pribram, K. H. The new neurology and the biology of emotion: A structural approach. *Amer. Psychol.,* 1967, 22, 830-838.

Prokasy, W. F. and J. F. Hall. Primary stimulus generalization. *Psychol. Rev.,* 1963, 70, 310-322.

Rapp, A. Experimental background of the problem of learning. *Classical Journal,* 1945 (May), 40, 467-480.

Razran, G. Stimulus generalization of conditioned responses. *Psychol. Bull.,* 1949, 46, 337-365.

Rickover, H. G. The world of the uneducated. *Sat. Eve. Post,* 1959 (November 28), 232, 19, 54, 57, 59.

Riesen, A. H., and J. Mellinger. Interocular transfer of habits in cats after alternating monocular visual experience. *J. comp. physiol. Psychol.,* 1956, 49, 516-520.

Rosanoff, M. A. Edison in his laboratory. *Harper's,* 1932, 165, 402-417.

Russell, W. A., and J. J. Jenkins. The complete Minnesota norms for responses to 100 words from the Kent-Rosanoff Word Association Test. Tech. Rep. No. 11, Contract N80NR-66216, Office of Naval Research and the University of Minnesota, 1954.

Russell, W. A., and L. H. Storms. Implicit verbal chaining in paired-associate learning. *J. exp. Psychol.,* 1955, 49, 287-293.

Sato, K. Psychotherapeutic implications of Zen. *Psychologia,* 1957, 1, 213-218.

Saugstad, P., and K. Raaheim. Problem-solving, past experience, and availability of functions. *Brit. J. Psychol.,* 1960, 51, 97-104.

Schiller, P. H. Innate constituents of complex responses in primates. *Psychol. Rev.,* 1952, 59, 177-191.

Seguín, Carlos Alberto, Instituto de Psiquietria Social, Lima, Peru. Personal communication.

Shayon, R. L. Let the debate be honest: Criticism of Admiral Rickover. *NEA Journal,* 1959, 48, 16-18.

Skinner, B. F. *Walden two.* New York: Macmillan, 1948.

――――. *Verbal behavior.* New York: Appleton-Century-Crofts, 1957.

References

———. Pigeons in a pelican. *Amer. Psychol.*, 1960, 15, 28-37.

———. *Contingencies of reinforcement: A theoretical analysis.* New York: Appleton-Century-Crofts, 1969.

Slamencka, N. J. An examination of trace storage in free recall. *J. exp. Psychol.*, 1968, 76, 504-513.

Smith, F. V. Toward definition of the stimulus situation for the approach response in the domestic chick. *Animal Behav.*, 1960, 8, 197-200. Also personal communication.

Sorenson, H. Adult ages as a factor in learning. *J. educ. Psychol.*, 1930, 21, 251-255.

Spence, K. W. The basis of solution by chimpanzees of the intermediate size problem. *J. exp. Psychol.*, 1942, 31, 257-271.

———, B. J. Underwood, and A. W. Melton. Symposium: Can the laws of learning be applied in the classroom? *Harvard educat. Rev.*, 1959, 29, 83-117.

Sperry, R. W. A modified concept of consciousness. *Psychol. Rev.*, 1969, 76, 532-536.

Spragg, S. D. S. Anticipatory responses in the maze. *J. comp. Psychol.*, 1934, 18, 51-73.

Street, R. F. *A Gestalt completion test.* New York: Teachers College, Columbia University, 1931.

Takemoto, T., T. Yatabe, S. Iwahara, and M. Ogawa. A developmental study of goal and entrance gradients in a unilinear maze in human subjects. *Psychologia*, 1957, 1, 30-36.

Taylor, D. W., P. C. Berry, and C. H. Block. Does group participation when using brainstorming facilitate or inhibit creative thinking? Tech. Rep. No. 1, ONR 150-166, 1957. Dept. Indust. Admin. Dept. Psychology, Yale University.

Terman, L. M. *Genetic studies of genius.* Vol. II. Stanford, Calif.: Stanford University Press, 1926.

Teuber, Hans-Lukas. The riddle of frontal lobe function in man. In J. M. Warren and K. Akert (Eds.), *The frontal granular cortex and behavior.* New York: McGraw-Hill, 1964.

Thorndike, E. L. *The psychology of learning.* Vol. II. New York: Teachers College, Columbia University, 1913.

———. *The fundamentals of learning.* New York: Teachers College, Columbia University, 1932.

———, and R. S. Woodworth. The influence of improvement in one mental function upon the efficiency of the other functions. *Psychol. Rev.*, 1901, 8, 247-261, 384-395, 553-564.

Tinbergen, N. *The study of instinct.* London: Oxford University Press, 1951.

Tinker, M. A., and F. L. Goodenough. Mirror reading as a method of analyzing factors involved in word perception. *J. educ. Psychol.*, 1931, 22, 493-502.

Titchener, E. B. *A textbook of psychology.* New York: Macmillan, 1921.

Tolman, E. C. *Purposive behavior in animals and men.* New York: D. Appleton-Century, 1932.

Travers, R. M. W. *Introduction to educational research.* New York: Macmillan, 1958.

Tulving, E., and Z. Pearlstone. Availability versus accessibility of information in memory for words. *J. verb. Learn. verb. Behav.*, 1966, 5, 381-391.

Tyler, R. Relation between recall and higher mental processes. In C. H. Judd (Ed.), *Education as cultivation of the higher mental processes.* New York: Macmillan, 1936.

Umemoto, T. Japanese studies in verbal learning and memory. *Psychologia*, 1959, 2, 1-19.

174 Watson, J. B. *Behavior: An introduction to comparative psychology.* New York: Holt, 1914.
175 Webster, R. G., and G. M. Haslerud. Influence on extreme peripheral vision of attention to a visual or auditory task. *J. exp. Psychol.*, 1964, 68, 269-272.
176 White, R. W. Motivation reconsidered: The concept of competence. *Psychol. Rev.*, 1959, 66, 297-333.
177 Wickelgren, W. A. Acoustic similarity and retroactive interference in short-term memory. *J. verb. Learn. verb. Behav.*, 1965, 4, 55-61.
178 Wiener, N. *The human use of human beings: Cybernetics and society.* Boston: Houghton Mifflin, 1950.
179 ———. *I am a mathematician.* Garden City, N.Y.: Doubleday & Company, 1956.
180 Yerkes, R. M., and D. N. Yerkes. Concerning memory in the chimpanzee. *J. comp. Psychol.*, 1928, 8, 237-271.
181 Zeigarnik, B. On finished and unfinished tasks. In W. D. Ellis (Ed.), *A source book of Gestalt psychology.* New York: Harcourt, Brace, 1938.
182 Zeiler, M. D. Transposition in adults with simultaneous and successive stimulus presentation. *J. exp. Psychol.*, 1964, 68, 103-107.

INDEX

Actualizing: dependence on skill, 90; different from insight, 123

Adams, D. K.: repeats Thorndike's problem box experiment on cats, 120

Adaptation level: contextual in sense organs and perceptual processes, 19

Adult: larger Apperceptive Mass of, 132; maintenance of Perceptual Future and growing edge, 132

Adult, older: needs to emphasize strengths and continue learning, 132

Adult education: need for new rationale in terms of projecscan, 131

After-learning: description of, 3; problems of, 3; from new theoretical stance, 5; defined, 106; process of, 126

Allport, F. G.: provides basis for structural and quantitative laws of perception, 102; neglected transfer problem, 102

Allport, G. W.: value of eidetic imagery for survival, 27; functional autonomy of ego, 149

Allusion: contextual relevance of, 87

Alpert, A.: relation of language to insights of children, 61; young children tested on Köhler insight problems, 95

Alternatives: from literal and creative transfer, 91

Alternatives, new: and problem of after-learning, 3; not available from free association mediation, 53; projective leap into undetermined Perceptual Future, 71; from set opposite that for good memory, 72; needs freedom of undetermined future, 76; made secure by retrieval cue in Apperceptive Mass, 88; suitability of in existing categories, 89; problem of, 112; from stereotyped memories, 116

Analogy: contextual relevance of, 87

Anticipation-projection: and new alternatives, 113; maintains relevance, 113

Apperceptive Mass: source of information complementary to that in environment, 16-17; illustrated in Figure *1*, 17, 20; outlined in Table *1*, 22; consists of independent centripetal whorls, 33, 148; no interconnections, 33-34; three contents of, 88; readiness of for quick imprinting, 93; and new perspectives, 95; increased by learning sets, 97-98; locus of nodal traces in whorls, 103; defined, 106; scanned by saccadic eye movements, 113-114; needs attention and consciousness for operation, 122; forays into for information, 122, 123, 126; development of, 127-128; problems

Index

Instinctive readiness: capable of exact and approximate cue elicitation, 97
Invariants. See E. J. Gibson, J. J. Gibson
Isomorphism, 23
Intent-to-retrieve: develops organization, 31; from reperception of attendant situation and vanishing information, 40, 41
Interocular transfer: studies of, 48

Jackson, P. O.: test of hypothesis making and production of variations, 65
Jacobson, C. F.: long response delays in monkeys, 32
James, W.: specious present, 21; similarity as post hoc, 121
Janney, J. E.: attributes specific transfer results to selection, 8
Jenkins, J. J.: mediated chains for transfer, 52; Minnesota norms for Kent-Rosanoff list, 112
Johdai, K.: effect of change of perception on behavior, 15
Judd, C. H.: mathematics and language as transferable school subjects, 13; criticized theory of identical elements, 47, 57; differential value of principle for learning and transfer, 57; better transfer requires appropriate learning conditions, 58; principles not always transferable, 117; educational implications, 125

Kay, H.: silent reading as witchcraft, 71
Klüver, H.: child's manipulation after delayed report of eidetic imagery, 27, 37
Koch, S.: theorists need to state assumptions and permit tests, 101
Koffka, K.: closure of forms, 29; tensions higher in intent-to-retrieve than when node is reached, 94
Knowledge: application of, 4; incomprehensibility of unless renewed, 4; social, 36; available and relevant for time of change, 150
Köhler, W.: isomorphism, 23; insight as new relationship of means and goal, 29; experiments on insight with chimpanzees, 29, 60-62, 76, 85, 90, 97, 123; transposition experiment with

hens, 50; whether transposition similar to insight, 96
Kolers, P. A.: language experiments of, 26
Konorski, J., 116
Korzybski, A.: man as time-binding animal, 76
Krech, I. (Krechevsky): experiments on hypothesis behavior in rats, 62-63, 96
Kuo, Z. Y.: kittens raised with rats, 122

Lashley, K. S.: criterion of learning in some rat experiments, 3; criticized stimulus generalization as lack of discrimination, 49
Lawrence, D. H.: alternatives presented before and after exposure of word, 80
Learning: not difficult, 4; lowers threshold, 18; can change adaptation level, 21; theories of accept identical elements and expect little transfer, 55; changes discriminability and availability, 103; operationally defined, 110; artificial separation from perception, 126. See also Incidental learning, Original learning
Lehman, H. C.: creative work only in early maturity, 66, 154
Leibowitz, H. W.: epigraph, 117
Liberal arts college: problems of in changing world, 132; old rationale of, 132; innovations without foundation in theory, 132; most necessary kind of education in changing world, 133
Limen: low for danger and defense, 16; usually high except for moment when stimulated, 16
Literal retrieval: and projecscan relapses, 111-112
Literal transfer: separated from creative transfer, 5; undermined by divorce of meaning and transfer, 51; from outer shell of whorl mistaken for nodal core, 54; on response side nothing new for bisymmetrical organism, 54; perseveration as stereotyped response, 55; based on identical elements, 57; avoids higher mental processes, 57; small in amount, 57; as blind alley, 150. See also Creative transfer, Projecscan
Longtime memory: and immediate